Opening the Scriptures
Faith Through the Year

Continuum
London and New York

Continuum
The Tower Building, 11 York Road, London SE1 7NX
370 Lexington Avenue, New York NY 10017-6503

First published 2001

British Library Cataloguing-in-Publication Data
A catalogue record for this book is available from the British Library.

ISBN 0-8264-4990-5

Designed and typeset by Paston Prepress, Beccles, Suffolk
Printed and bound in Great Britain by TJ International Limited, Padstow, Cornwall

CONTENTS

Introduction

All the addresses in this book were originally given to students at Exeter College, Oxford, during four and a half recent years when I held a part-time office as the College Catechist. I am told I was the first woman, the first layperson, and the first Catholic to fulfil this ancient function at the traditional little college in the heart of the city of dreaming spires.

The essence of the post is to preach twice a term at evensong, which at Exeter is a gloriously classic occasion with a thundering French organ and an exceptionally talented choir led by an undergraduate organ scholar. It is a formal and reverent time of worship, affording abundant inner space for quiet reflection, and drawing to a close with a sermon delivered in formal style from a lectern set between the two rows of choir stalls.

People have differing ideas of the aims of preaching, with some people promoting the stirring sermon and others the learned one. But both aspects are important. What I aimed to do, in each of these addresses, was to stretch the brains of my student listeners as well as to touch their hearts. A homily that tries to swing the emotions while offering no intellectual stimulation, I thought, would be unworthy of the fertile and exploratory minds of clever young people. It could only contribute to a growing dichotomy between their religious life and their intellectual life: their brains mature while their faith remains childlike. So I always tried to tell them something they did not already know, or to offer them an idea that they would not have heard from anyone else.

At the same time, a sermon that tries to be original or clever, while failing to arouse a response of faith and love in the listener, misses the point. I knew I was there to preach the

Christian faith with fidelity – a faith I happen to hold with conviction – and not to ride my own personal hobby-horses. So one guide I employed was the lectionary: if I preached on the readings of the day, rather than selecting my favourite passages of the Bible, then I would have a better chance of presenting a balanced picture of the Judeo-Christian faith, and a lesser risk of becoming obsessed with my own preoccupations. The backdrop of the church's year provides the necessary spread of themes: it is the framework for presenting the Christian faith for the half-believer and the searcher as well as for the fervently committed.

Perhaps the best pattern for the preacher, which none of us can reach except fleetingly, is the example of the stranger on the way to Emmaus. 'Were not our hearts burning within us', said his listeners, '... while he was opening the scriptures to us?' Here the speaker conveys both light and warmth, and the listeners set off enthusiastically, with new insight into their mission (Luke 24.32–3).

I was grateful for the opportunity given me to communicate the good news of the Christian gospel, and I hoped there might be something in my words that would make my listeners glad to be Christian and inspire them to go out and put their faith into practice. With just a little editing, I now offer my reflections to a wider audience.

BEGINNINGS

CHAPTER ONE

Welcome

Ruth 1; Philippians 3.1–16

In Oxford, as in most cities, the Christian community is enormously varied. It ranges from the evangelical to the ritualistic, from Reformed worship to Orthodox liturgy, from churches prominent in social action (such as the care of asylum-seekers) to groups that promote a contemplative style of worship (such as Taizé chant), from the freedom and silence of the Quaker meeting to the more charismatic hymn-singing of ecumenical student events, from the big congregations of undergraduates that gather in chaplaincies to the little meetings in students' rooms for Bible study, from the buzz of discussion about controversial contemporary issues to the elegant formality and beautiful music of Book of Common Prayer evensong. There is space for every type of spiritual searcher to find a home – perhaps several homes, for we can enjoy and celebrate the diversity of all these types of Christian celebration without having to settle for any mushy compromise between them.

Finding a home is crucial for those who arrive in a new place. However much they are looking forward to the privileges and excitement of a new college or a new job, new friends or new lifestyle, there is also the apprehension that they may not quite fit in. Today's readings are directed particularly towards people with that apprehension, towards those who are joining a new group and wondering if they belong. The readings speak to the needs of first-year students, and of anyone else who is making a new start in a new place.

In the epistle to the Philippians, Paul speaks on one of his familiar themes – the question of circumcision. He was speaking to men who had adopted the God of the Jews and the Messiah of the Jews, and who were now struggling with the question of whether they should also undergo the initiation of the Jews – circumcision. They did not want to feel constant outsiders, marginal adherents to the new Christian faith. Should they be circumcised? This was a really major question in those days, the equivalent of the women's ordination question for that era, or even bigger, an issue on which Jesus had given no explicit personal authority for a change in the ancient practice.

It aroused very strong feelings, with one group pointing out that Jesus was circumcised and obeyed the law and that he had said not one jot or tittle would pass away from it. And so they concluded that 'unless you are circumcised according to the custom of Moses, you cannot be saved' (Acts 15.1). There was much heated debate in the council of Jerusalem before the early Christian church made a decisive and clear judgement on it: circumcision was not necessary.

But Jesus was also the 'light to lighten the gentiles', as Simeon said in Luke 2.32, and as we sing in the *Nunc Dimittis* at evensong. It was Paul who was the most articulate and forceful spokesman on behalf of the gentiles and the uncircumcised, even though he himself was one of the circumcised. The main argument was not from past tradition but from the contemporary experience of the church – that the grace of God is evidently poured out on to the uncircumcised. He argued in Romans that 'real circumcision is a matter of the heart' (Romans 2.29).

In today's passage from Philippians Paul uses quite strong language to rid his hearers of even the residual suspicion that they would be better to accept circumcision, by warning them off the physical practice. He says, 'beware of those who mutilate the flesh!' He calls those who press for it 'dogs' and 'evil workers'. 'For it is we who are the circumcision, who worship in the Spirit of God and boast in Christ Jesus and have no confidence in the flesh' (Philippians 3.3).

What he achieved was to reassure those who were not quite sure how fully they belonged to God's chosen people that they really did belong. And so those who are not quite sure how fully they belong to the new group they have joined, should take heart. They need not let it all overwhelm them. They need not let the strain of high expectations make them feel marginal. There are people to help, people to turn to inside the Christian community as well as outside. And there is the witness of Paul and the early Christian community, saying: don't feel marginalized – you belong.

The first reading, from Ruth, is about a woman facing the same question: how to belong to God's chosen people when she was born a foreigner. Ruth was a Moabite, and Moabites were not well thought of. They were said to be descended from the incestuous union of Lot and one of his daughters when he was drunk (Genesis 19.30–8), and Deuteronomy 23.3 instructs that 'no . . . Moabite shall be admitted to the assembly of the Lord'. And yet Ruth, though a Moabite, becomes one of the great biblical women – a woman of inspiring initiative who has a whole book named after her, even if a very short book. You have just heard a quarter of it, and it is well worth reading the remaining three chapters before you go to bed tonight. Then you will read how she made herself look and smell beautiful and went to lie on the threshing floor (where prostitutes would often lie, as we learn from Hosea 9.1). She lay down stealthily next to Boaz and uncovered his genitals (the Old Testament uses the euphemism of 'feet' for genitals), and asked him to spread his cloak over them both. When I hear people urging us to follow the biblical teaching on sexual relations I sometimes wonder what version of the Bible they are reading.

In the first chapter of Matthew, Jesus' genealogy is traced, and four women are mentioned there, of whom Ruth is one. The others are Tamar, who posed as a prostitute and seduced her father-in-law (Genesis 38.15–19); Rahab, who was a gentile prostitute from Jericho (Joshua 2.2); and Bathsheba, who committed adultery with David (2 Samuel 11.2–5). Why Matthew should have chosen such a group of women to establish Jesus' pedigree is an intriguing question, for each is known for her irregular sexual relations. The ancient Fathers used to say they were sinners in need of salvation by Christ, but the answer more often favoured by today's biblical scholars is that they were misunderstood but righteous women whose history prepares the reader for the irregular conception of Jesus.

Ruth does her bold, seductive act in order to have a son after the death of her husband, Naomi's son, in order to keep his name alive. We may add that in that society, women could not survive unless they had male relatives: the most important role of a woman was to bear sons, who could inherit. The story has a happy ending, and Ruth is praised for her loyalty, her love and her determination, and she is said to be worth more to Naomi than seven sons.

But in the first chapter of Ruth, I want to draw attention to another point. Ruth is urged to follow her sister-in-law back 'to her people and to her gods'. She refuses, and clings to a new people with their one God, telling Naomi, 'your people shall be my people, and your God my God'. She defies all the Jewish suspicion of gentiles, and of Moabites in particular, and refuses to give up, refuses to be made to feel she does not belong. That is an example to undergraduates, or anyone else, feeling ill at ease over finding their feet.

As Christians, our Jewish relative is not Naomi, but Jesus. In following him, in cleaving inseparably to membership of his family, we too can refuse to give up. We too can love the Jewish people as our own nation, whether we share with them the circumcision or not. We too can scorn all anti-Semitism wherever it reappears. We too can refuse to allow anyone to be made to feel marginal by reason of their race or their sex or the newness of their arrival. We too can make Ruth's words our own, addressing them now not to Naomi, but to Jesus, in perfect trust, not knowing what bold acts that loyalty will lead us to in years to come:

> Where you go, I will go;
> where you lodge, I will lodge;
> your people shall be my people,
> and your God my God. (Ruth 1.16)

CHAPTER TWO

The Time is Now

Ezekiel 12.21–8; 1 Peter 1.3–21

The readings we have heard this evening have prompted me to think about time – special times and ordinary times, privileged times and lax times, the tension between the now and the not yet of salvation. The Millennium is a prime example of a special time – 2000 years after the supposed birth of Christ. There are many other special times in the life of each one of us, periods of opportunity which we hope not to waste, such as the three or four years spent at college when young, or a long visit abroad, the beginning of a marriage, the arrival of grand-children, or the start of retirement.

When we read Ezekiel, written some six centuries before Christ, he too is wrestling with the question of a special time. Ezekiel had long proclaimed the imminence of divine judge-ment, yet the days passed on and nothing happened. People would say 'the days are prolonged and every vision comes to nothing'.

Ezekiel tried to instil a new sense of urgency, saying the day is close for a fulfilment of his visions, when the word of God will no longer be delayed.

The second reading, from the first epistle of Peter, wrestles in a different way with the same problem, the problem of those living in ordinary times who feel a certain distance from the immediacy of God's word. The epistle is addressed to those in what is called the *diaspora*, or the dispersion, that is, those who are scattered away from the Holy Land, the church spread through the world.

We too are in that *diaspora*, and the further we plunge into secular society, the more thoroughly we put ourselves into the *diaspora*. Mission is important, but the difficulty is to go on feeling a strong bond of unity with the central branches of the vine from which we receive spiritual nourishment. The challenge is to maintain a keen sense of the privileged places and the special times when we have felt close to God, as we become immersed in the everyday world.

The author of 1 Peter is writing to people who never personally met Jesus. Because we too are in the same position, I have always felt these words to be extraordinarily helpful: 'Although you have not seen him, you love him; and even though you do not see him now, you believe in him and rejoice with an indescribable and glorious joy' (1 Peter 1.8). What he says applies as much to us today as it did to the people he was writing to, or more so: although *we* have not seen Jesus, *we* love him. It is not just a matter of fantasy; a personal relationship is possible because of the very real way in which Jesus continues to be alive.

There is always a tendency to feel second-best because we do not belong to those privileged to see Jesus face to face, to hear his words spoken by the man himself, to be physically present as Peter was in that wonderful verse at the beginning of the second epistle of Peter – 'We ourselves heard this voice come from heaven, while we were with him on the holy mountain' (2 Peter 1.18). Yet the writer of the epistle wants to instil a sense of specialness, even to those who are feeling very special. He is writing to people who, he says, 'have had to suffer various trials', and is reminding them of the promise of their 'imperishable, undefiled, and unfading' inheritance (1 Peter 1.4, 6).

It is the same message that Jesus himself gave when he urged people to 'keep awake therefore, for you know neither the day nor the hour' (Matthew 25.13), backing it up with the parable of foolish virgins who let their oil lamps run out because they had to wait so long (Matthew 25.1–12). Some devotional traditions tell us to live every day as though it were our last; in practice that is hard to do, because it feels like pretending. Someone who has just lost something of irreplaceable value – who has been blown up by a mine and lost a leg for example, or who has lost a girlfriend or a boyfriend, lost a parent or lost a child – also has a sense of regret that they had not lived to the full every day up to then, rejoicing and giving thanks for their health or for the lives of those they loved. Yet the sense of specialness of the ordinary does not come easily.

I want to mention two very different modern writings which have come to different conclusions on the idea of a special time. One is the post-Christian feminist theologian, Daphne Hampson, who spoke in the College shortly before I became Catechist. The other is the South African *Kairos* document.

Daphne Hampson describes herself as a post-Christian because she comes from Christian culture but rejects its faith. The kernel of her intellectual difficulties lies in the idea of a special time, a privileged time. Her position, she writes in *Theology and Feminism* (Basil Blackwell, 1990), is that 'God is equally available to people in all times and places ... that is to say I deny that there could be a particular revelation of God in any one age, which thenceforth becomes normative for all others.' She says 'I am simply denying that God ... could intervene in human history, or be revealed through particular events in history, or through a particular person, in a way in which God is not potentially present to us in and through all acts and persons.'

I think there is a sense in which Daphne Hampson is right, and a sense in which she is wrong. We all need to recover a sense of urgency. Those who live in the ordinary times, who don't see Jesus, who live in the *diaspora*, are not second-best. Those who have never heard of Jesus are not excluded from salvation.

Yet at the same time, to call every age and culture equal in terms of God's revelation seems to be contrary to our experience. Our knowledge of God comes to us through particular times, special places, unique people. We cherish particular moments of religious experience that feel quite intensely out of the ordinary. We go on pilgrimage, to Taizé, or to India, or to wherever speaks to us. We come to faith through the influence of a person or people we admire. All times are special, but there is no doubt that some are more special than others. The kingdom is now, and to come. We are (in the words of 1 Peter) both in exile and already ransomed.

The *Kairos* document was produced in South Africa in 1985 and in 1995 its tenth anniversary was celebrated. It spoke of a special time – in biblical Greek a *kairos* – in the history of the nation. It began:

> The time has come. The moment of truth has arrived. South Africa has been plunged into a crisis that is shaking the foundations . . . .

And it continues;

> This is the KAIROS, the moment of grace and opportunity, the favourable time in which God issues a challenge to decisive action. It is a dangerous time because, if this opportunity is missed, and allowed to pass by, the loss for the Church, for the Gospel, and for all the people of South Africa will be immeasurable. Jesus wept over Jerusalem.

And again:

> A crisis is a moment of truth that shows us up for what we really are. There will be no place to hide and no way of pretending to be what we are not in fact.

This is fine stuff, worthy of Ezekiel, and how wonderful it is that the *kairos* was not missed, that the challenge to decisive action in South Africa was taken. Christianity is a religion that stresses the importance of the historical moment. It mattered that South Africa threw off the chains of oppression. It mattered that Jesus lived, and died.

That is why in the end I don't agree with Daphne Hampson. All times are special in their way, yet there are privileged moments.

So there is an invitation, at the turn of the Millennium, at the beginning of the academic year, at the start of any new period of promise, as there was in the time of Ezekiel, as there was at the time of Jesus, as there was in the epistle of Peter, and as there was in 1985 in South Africa, to seize the privileged moment. *Carpe diem*: pluck the day. Live life to the full. In the words of 1 Peter: 'Therefore prepare your minds for action; discipline yourselves; set all your hope on the grace that Jesus Christ will bring you when he is revealed' (1 Peter 1.13).

Or in words commonly attributed to Nelson Mandela, though the attribution has been challenged:

Our deepest fear is not that we are inadequate. Our deepest fear is that we are powerful beyond measure. It is our light, not our darkness, that most frightens us. We ask ourselves, who am I to be brilliant, gorgeous, talented and fabulous? Actually, who are you not to be? You are a child of God.

CHAPTER THREE

The Creation of Women and Men

Genesis 2.4–25; Mark 10.1–16

This chapter from Genesis is one of the readings that I and my husband Peter chose for our wedding, so you will understand it is a passage of which I am particularly fond. I remember being flooded with wedding nerves which made me particularly susceptible to the power of the text, so that my voice trembled and I nearly broke down. It was a great relief to get to the boring bit about the rivers, so that I had time to regain my composure.

About ten years later, I was at another wedding in Magdalen College chapel, and again Genesis 2 was chosen. At the end of the nuptial mass I said to my neighbour what a lovely reading it was, and she said on the contrary she thought it was utterly appalling, and she was shocked it was used as a text for a marriage. The man is the centre of everything, she said, for he is the first to be created, and the woman is derived from him – made out of his rib – and given to him as his helper. What a bad foundation for two people to build a lifetime relationship on.

Can the Genesis text be defended? I think it can be, up to a point, and the chief grounds for its defence are highlighted in the translation we are using this evening, on which I should say a few words of explanation. The translation is called *At the Start ... Genesis made New* (Leuvense Schrijversaktie, 1992, distributed in the UK by Sheffield Academic Press). It has been done

by an Englishwoman living in Belgium, called Mary Phil
Korsak, whose main work has been in teaching translators
and interpreters, but her theological interest led her to make
this translation of Genesis from the Hebrew.

The translation principle she has used is a surprising one: it
is to translate every word absolutely literally. The result is
surprisingly poetic, and at the same time we have the satisfaction of knowing we are as close as we can be to the original.
Every Hebrew word is rendered by one, and one only, English
word, without varying the translation according to the context.
Maximum use is made of the kind of word play that is found in
the original, and original sentence structures are echoed.

Mary Phil Korsak is not the first to work on these principles.
She tells us that Aquila did the same, in the first half of the
second century, when he translated the Hebrew Bible into
Greek. His translation was said to have been appreciated by
Greek-speaking Jews, and was admired by Origen and Jerome.
During this century Martin Buber and Franz Rosenzweig
picked up the method again with their German Bible, and
André Chouraqui did something similar in French, and Mirja
Ronning in the Finnish. A group of scholars known as the
Amsterdam school is working along the same lines in Dutch.

Here is her rendering of Genesis 2.4–25:

> These are the breedings of the skies and the earth
> at their creation
>
> On the day YHWH Elohim made earth and skies
> no shrub of the field was yet in the earth
> no plant of the field had yet sprouted
> for YHWH Elohim had not made it rain on the earth
> and there was no groundling to serve the ground
> But a surge went up from the earth
> and gave drink to all the face of the ground
>
> YHWH Elohim formed the groundling, soil of the ground
> He blew into its nostrils the blast of life
> and the groundling became a living soul
>
> YHWH Elohim planted a garden in Eden in the east
> There he set the groundling he had formed

YHWH Elohim made sprout from the ground
all trees attractive to see and good for eating
the tree of life in the middle of the garden
and the tree of the knowing of good and bad

A river goes out in Eden to give drink to the garden
From there it divides and becomes four heads
The name of the first is Pishon
It winds through all the land of Havilah
where there is gold
The gold of that land is good
bdellium is there and onyx stone
The name of the second river is Gihon
It winds through all the land of Cush
The name of the third river is Tigris
It goes east of Asshur
The fourth river is Euphrates

YHWH Elohim took the groundling
and set it to rest in the garden of Eden
to serve it and keep it
YHWH Elohim commanded the groundling, saying
Of every tree of the garden eat! you shall eat
but of the tree of the knowing of good and bad
you shall not eat
for on the day you eat of it
die! you shall die

YHWH Elohim said
It is not good for the groundling to be alone
I will make for it a help as its counterpart
YHWH Elohim formed out of the ground
all beasts of the field, all fowl of the skies
and brought them to the groundling
to see what it would call them
Whatever the groundling called to each living soul
that is its name
The groundling called names for all the cattle
for all fowl of the skies, for all beasts of the field
But for a groundling it found no help as its counterpart

> YHWH Elohim made a swoon fall upon the groundling
> it slept
> He took one of its sides
> and closed up the flesh in its place
> YHWH Elohim built the side
> he had taken from the groundling into woman
> He brought her to the groundling
> The groundling said
> > This one this time
> > is bone from my bones
> > flesh from my flesh
> > This one shall be called wo-man
> > for from man
> > she has been taken this one
> So a man will leave his father and his mother
> he will cling to his wo-man
> and they will become one flesh
> The two of them were naked
> the groundling and his woman
> they were not ashamed

One of the most striking points about her rendering of Genesis 2 is the use of 'groundling' where other translations have 'man', and here of course we are beginning to address the objection raised by my friend in Magdalen College chapel. Mary Phil Korsak has rejected 'man' for two reasons. Firstly, it fails to express the linguistic relation in Hebrew between the man/groundling (*adam*) and the ground (*adamah*). So the RSV (Revised Standard Version) has 'there was no man to till the ground', where Korsak has 'there was no groundling to serve the ground'. The New Revised Standard Version, which has a moderate amount of inclusive language, is perhaps more accurate in having 'there was no one to till the ground'. But even the NRSV has 'God formed man from the dust of the ground', while Korsak says God 'formed the groundling, soil of the ground'.

Korsak's other reason for using 'groundling' is that Hebrew has two words customarily translated 'man'. *Adam*, which means a human person, and *ish*, which means man in the sense of a male person. And so Korsak is able to distinguish between the verses where the Hebrew talks of humanity in general, and those where the male sex is specified. In today's reading we have groundling – with the gender neutral pronoun 'it' rather than 'he' – right up to the end of verse 23. Then a distinction is needed between the sexes for a wordplay in both Hebrew and English between *ish* and *ishah*, or 'man' and 'wo-man':

> This one shall be called wo-man
> for from man
> she has been taken this one

We can see from this that the sexism is much less acute in the Hebrew than in the English versions we are familiar with. It is the groundling – male or female – who is formed from the soil of the ground. It is the groundling – male or female – who is created first of all living things. (Note that Genesis 2 differs from the story in Genesis 1, which is a completely separate account of creation, by a different writer, where human beings are created last. In both cases we are the summit of creation, in the first chapter last – the culmination; in the second chapter first – the priority.) Much of the male primacy that people have been accustomed to reading into this text actually derives from the inaccuracy of using one English word for two Hebrew ones.

However, though we can blame translation for much of the sexism, I do not think in the end we can exculpate the text entirely. As the chapter progresses we find that the groundling is in the end assumed to be male, as it almost imperceptibly merges into the man, who greets the woman as the one taken 'from man'. The assumption of male priority is less marked, but it is not entirely absent. It reminds us of practices even in our own day which treat women in terms of their relationship to men, like calling a woman Mrs. John Smith, or introducing her as 'John Smith's wife'.

To meet this problem, we need to ask if the sexist element is the point of the story, or if it is rather the cultural clothing for another point. Old Testament writers thought, spoke and acted in a context where sexual inequality was taken for granted, as sexual equality is taken for granted today. We do the texts an injustice to derive from them messages of male headship which were never intentionally planted there.

What then is the real message of the text? I think we need to step back a bit from our dry analysis, trying to excuse the Bible from error, and get in touch with the immense power of the story. The garden of Eden is an idea that has held excitement and enticement for people of all ages, from *Paradise Lost*, the poem of Milton, to *Paradise News*, the novel of David Lodge, which he prefaces with a quotation from a guidebook to Hawaii: 'The earthly paradise! Don't you want to go to it? Why of course!' Sun, leisure, beautiful trees, delicious fruit, harmony with nature, harmony with others, harmony with self . . . it is a dream that never leaves the human heart.

The beautiful garden is an image evoked on a relaxation tape I use when I find it hard to get to sleep.

> In your imagination, create a peaceful garden. Visualize without straining, as many details as you can ... the sounds, movement, colours, and scents .... You open the gate and step inside ... leaving all negative thoughts outside. Only positive thoughts of peace, optimism, happiness and contentment are allowed in. You take a seat. You feel very peaceful. There is no work to be done .... Visualize the plants growing in the garden, some covering the ground and many colourful flowers and shrubs and trees.

Genesis 2 is the source and the touchstone of this universal longing, this utopia. It is evoked again in the book of Isaiah:

> The wolf shall live with the lamb,
> the leopard shall lie down with the kid . . . .
> They will not hurt or destroy
> on all my holy mountain;
> for the earth will be full of the knowledge of the Lord
> as the waters cover the sea. (Isaiah 11.6, 9)

There is the real message of the Garden of Eden: it is not just harmony with nature and between man and woman, but a place drenched with the awareness of God. In nature we find God.

We can draw out another valuable insight from this story. The first creation story, Genesis 1, is sometimes criticized by creation theologians such as, for example, Matthew Fox, for promoting a dangerous idea of stewardship, for God says to the humans: 'have dominion over the fish of the sea and over the birds of the air and over every living thing that moves upon the earth' (Genesis 1.28). (Korsak has 'Govern the fish of the sea, the fowl of the skies/every beast that creeps on the earth'.) Of this dominion, it is said, is born the kind of arrogance, the anthropocentric – that is human-centred – arrogance, that has led to the exploitation of the planet out of human greed.

This may be a misreading of Genesis 1 – and I think it is – but in any case the second creation story corrects the picture, particularly in Mary Phil Korsak's version. The groundling is set in the garden 'to serve it and keep it'. (The NRSV has 'till' for 'serve'.) Whereas in Genesis 1 our responsibility is to 'govern' creation, in Genesis 2 it is to 'serve' creation. In fact the two are not incompatible, but any attitude of environmental irresponsibility is clearly sinful by this account. If we squander the nature that we are set to serve, we will forfeit the beauty of the garden as a perfect place to dwell, and will earn pain and thorn and thistle in its place.

There is one more thing that needs to be said, which will put into context the accusations of sexism by overshadowing them with a much more striking message. The point of the relationship between the woman and man is not dependence and priority, but love. The groundling cries out with joy and wonder.

> This one this time
> is bone from my bones
> flesh from my flesh

And so the two became one flesh. This is the universal cry of lovers – that is of those who truly love each other to the full – as they stand before each other in their nakedness. It is the kind of love that recognizes not just that we *ought* to treat each other as we would like to be treated, but that we really feel ourselves to be one. It is a recognition of a physical identification that overrides even the existing ties of blood-relationship:

> So a man will leave his father and his mother
> he will cling to his wo-man
> and they will become one flesh

It is a message to be borne in mind especially, perhaps, by those who stand at the mid-point between leaving parents behind and embracing another as their own flesh in a new family union.

What message could be more profound, more radical, more powerful or more daring than this message: that the naked joy of lovers, of true lovers, is a gift blessed by God, to be enjoyed in harmony with God, because it is for this that God has made us? We may speak slightingly and jokingly at times of the earthly paradise of sun, sand and sex. But behind it lies a truth, a half-forgotten memory of all our human race, of what life could be like if lived truly in harmony with creation, in union with each other, and in the knowledge of God.

CHAPTER FOUR

Remembrance Sunday and Diana

Isaiah 10.33 – 11.9; Revelation 21.1–7

As a nation we have not been very good in recent years at Remembrance Sunday. Fearful of militarist overtones, reluctant to dwell on death, unaccustomed to being silent and still, we have felt some discomfort over this recollection of the war dead.

But whatever our views on war, we can all remember. We can remember those dead on both sides, and those killed in all wars, in all parts of the world. We can remember those left behind bereaved. There is no excuse for avoiding these heavy memories.

Without those two world wars the world would be a different place, in some ways perhaps better, in some ways worse. In the period running up to the Millennium the Vatican spent some time considering what sort of apology it owed to the Jews; but it is appropriate to recall that without the sacrifice of those who died in the Second World War, there might be no Jews left to apologize to.

As I took part in the silence earlier today, another thought struck me, which I will share with you, unfashionable as it is. War is not only about people of one generation dying for their children. It is also about men dying for women. Though perhaps it is true to say men more than women make war, it is also true to say that men more than women give their lives in war. That is something humbling, something worth remembering.

There is of course more than one way of giving your life for others. They also gave their lives who now suffer from Gulf War syndrome, and that affects many thousands of veterans. Which is worse: a premature bloody death when all is quickly over? Or a bloodless, lingering living death? It is not easy to say.

As a nation we have been bad at remembering the dead, until, I think, the death of Princess Diana. The extraordinary phenomenon of our reactions to her death took us all by surprise. C. S. Lewis spoke of being *Surprised by Joy*, but the end of the summer of 1997 gave us a new experience of being Surprised by Grief.

Tom Wright, the Dean of Lichfield and former chaplain of Worcester College, Oxford, preached a sermon at that time in which he suggested:

> Our society is not good at expressing grief, or coming to terms with it. Funerals and cremations are often brief, perfunctory, and impersonal. Mourners are commended for 'being brave': in other words for suppressing the natural, God-given emotion of grief .... As a result, many people carry around unresolved grief which they don't know what to do with. Suddenly Diana has given us all a chance to express it.

And so our nation, which has felt so reluctant about Remembrance Day ceremonies, so ambivalent about blood-red poppies and so reluctant to stand still in silence, rediscovered in the Diana event a lost chord. Before Diana's heavy, lead-lined coffin left the west door of Westminster Abbey, the whole nation stood still for one minute of silence. For those watching on television, a gothic arch framed the motionless mourners; and then the picture of Diana herself, in the sad photograph that was used regularly on television after her death, was superimposed ghost-like upon the people beneath as if to say: she is watching us now.

It was a minute of such heavy and unspeakable grief that all the pain and misery of the world seemed to be unlocked through this icon of the people. Through having been a member of the royal family, Diana became a member of everyone's family, reminding us that we are indeed one family, so that it is wholly appropriate to grieve for someone we have never met. Those who wept, were weeping for their own mortality, and the mortality of all their sisters and brothers who die with much of their life wasted, whether their death is untimely or not. They were weeping too for those Diana loved and for whose sake she suffered, particularly those maimed by landmines.

To that grief at irreversible death, that waste of opportunities in a life snuffed out, that inconsolable pain at the agonies of dying and maiming and wounding, the scriptures speak with almost unbearable poignancy.

The verse of Isaiah 11 that most haunts me is the one with which tonight's reading ended: '... for the earth will be full of the knowledge of the Lord as the waters cover the sea' (Isaiah 11.9). It evokes the longing for God, the longing for the full knowledge of God to flood over us with an immensity like the ocean. This knowledge of God, 'as the waters cover the sea', comes, in Isaiah, with the gift of peace. The wolf shall lie down with the lamb, and the child shall put her hand over the adder's den, and they will not hurt or destroy in all God's holy mountain.

It is the peace for which people long when there is war, and more than the peace they long for. But it is no cheap peace. This is not the peace of those who agree to overlook their differences and make compromises in what they believe to be of fundamental importance. Rather, it is the peace that comes after the purging power of justice. With righteousness shall God judge the poor, and God shall strike the earth with the rod of his mouth, and with the breath of God's lips shall evil be destroyed. The peace that God holds out as a promise to us is peace with justice, peace through justice, and especially peace through justice to the poor and the meek.

The passage from Revelation 21 is one that can easily move me to tears, simply by its promise that 'he will wipe every tear from their eyes'. So often, when someone else acknowledges the hurt we are feeling, we are enabled to feel that hurt more keenly, and to let the tears flow. And so we can let ourselves weep for all the unhealed hurt that we have ever suffered, and for all the unhealed hurt that we have ever inflicted. We can weep for the pain brought about by those we love most dearly, and especially for the pain brought about by the death of those we love most dearly.

As we remember the inconsolable grief of this world of war and tears and dying, and the incredible promises of the next world of peace and joy and justice, the gap between them may feel unbridgeable and the yearning to pass from one to the other unbearable. But there is a bridge, a bridge we cross, once again, by remembering.

On the night before he suffered, a man took bread and broke it, saying 'Take, eat, for this is my body, given for you; do this in remembrance of me.' And he took a cup and said, 'Drink, for this is my blood, poured out for you, for the forgiveness of sins.'

In remembering that death, we do more than grieve for mortality, more even than look forward to the promise of immortality. In remembering that death, we say 'Yes' to it, we accept the peace it won for us. We take it to ourselves, we eat it and we drink it, we carry our cross with Jesus, are buried and rise with him. At one and the same time we take to ourselves the cross and the resurrection, and the necessary connection between the two, the bridge that passes from death to life.

In this bungling world we try to do our best to get things right, and sometimes we get things horribly, horrifically wrong. Were the two world wars justified? Were the more recent wars in the Falklands and the Gulf justified? Is modern war ever justified? God only knows. But let us not shirk from at least remembering those who gave their lives for their people, rightly or wrongly making the ultimate sacrifice, meaning to do well. And I would want to do more, I would want to say 'Thank you'.

But let us all say 'Thank you' with undivided confidence as we remember the man who gave his life for his people, to take from us the deepest enemy to our peace – our sins. That was indeed the necessary sacrifice, the death that justifies – the death that brings peace with justice. Because of that death, in which we seek to bury all our deaths, we now can say:

> Death will be no more;
> mourning and crying and pain will be no more,
> for the first things have passed away. (Revelation 21.4)

LOOKING TOWARDS
CHRISTMAS

CHAPTER FIVE

Prisoners' Sunday and Liberation

Exodus 2.23 – 3.20; John 6.24–40

Today is celebrated by many churches as Prisoners' Sunday, when we remember those whose lives are reduced in the most extreme way possible, through the loss of their freedom, and whose fates are so easily forgotten about, because we do not see them. (To forget them is indeed some people's intention: we hear talk of locking criminals up and throwing away the key.) Today we pray for prisoners, and we pray also for ourselves and our own attitudes towards prisoners: we pray that we may not forget; we pray that we may be able to forgive – not excuse but forgive; we pray that we may live in joyful thankfulness for our liberties.

An acute reminder of how much we 'booky' people have to be thankful for is given in the account by a Chilean prisoner, Herman Váldez, of his feelings of jubilation when he got hold of a single sheet of newspaper:

> I spread the magnificent loot on my bed and quickly worked out how I would enjoy it. It consisted of four pages from the magazine section of the weekend paper – three pages of advertisements and a back page of crossword puzzles, chess and stamp news. How lucky I was. There were no less than three crossword puzzles. Here was a week's reading material at least. One crossword puzzle every other day, and in between a page of advertisements. Every day for a week I had something to look forward to.

I read the Births and the Marriages, and even the Deaths.
So the world had not stood still. I read the 'Cars for Sale'
and the 'We Want to Swop' columns. For one glorious
week I dipped into my treasure, each day carefully
restoring it to its hiding place under the mattress or in
my clothes. Special savour was given to the crossword
puzzles by the fact that I had to fill them in with a pin and
marmite. (*Diary of a Chilean Concentration Camp*, Victor
Gollancz, 1975)

That should be enough to send you all back to your reading
lists with gusto. We do not realise how lucky we are.

We pray that we may not forget those who are imprisoned.
One person who does not forget is God, and that is the point
made in today's famous reading from the book of Exodus, the
story of the burning bush. Talk of the fire of the Spirit can
become clichéd, when it is emptied of practical content; but if
we look at the context of the burning bush we find that these are
flames of passionate remembrance, even anger, as God hears
the cries of his people imprisoned within Egypt, and burns with
zeal to set them free.

The Israelites groaned under their slavery, and cried out.
Out of the slavery their cry for help rose up to God. God
heard their groaning, and God remembered his covenant
with Abraham, Isaac, and Jacob. God looked upon the
Israelites, and God took notice of them. (Exodus 2.23–5)

It could hardly be said more emphatically, more times over,
that God does not forget his children who are imprisoned or
oppressed. So God focuses his passionate determination to
change the situation in the burning bush – a bush that burns
creatively, not destructively, that is not consumed by its flames.
And along with the sheer wonder and awesomeness of the
divine presence – a presence that makes Moses take off his
shoes in respect and hide his face in fear, and that is summed
up in that famous and enigmatic name 'I am who I am' – is
one single message: 'I have observed the misery of my people
... I have heard their cry ... I know their sufferings', and most

importantly, 'I have come down to deliver them' (Exodus 3.7–8).

This event of deliverance, the exodus, which gives its name to the book, is one of the most important events of the entire Bible. From slavery into freedom is *the* Christian message. The deliverance of the people of God who pass from death in Egypt, through the waters of the Red Sea, to a new life in the promised land, is picked up again in Christian belief by the deliverance of the people of God, who pass from the death of sin, through the waters of baptism, to the new and eternal life of Christ.

This much is well known and well accepted. But over the centuries a distortion appeared, which cut away at the foundations of the original biblical teaching. The distortion was to reduce the message of salvation history, played out in the Bible through a sequence of real historical events, to a spiritualized message, cut off from its rooting in actual historical reality. The exodus came to stand for a purely spiritual event, almost indeed a psychological event, devoid of political or social expressions. The new life of Christ came to be seen as just something after death, so that life in this world did not matter. Whatever pain or injustice, imprisonment or deprivation people might suffer in this world, would be made up to them after death, when they got to heaven.

And so the critics of Christianity, particularly Marxist critics, came to attack the idea of 'pie in the sky', and 'religion as the opium of the people' – opium in the sense that it deadened the natural reactions of outrage and struggle that an oppressed people has every right to feel: don't worry if you live in hunger and homelessness now; it will all come right in the end when you get to heaven; so shut up.

Now there is not much doubt that these critics had some justification, and Christianity had to some extent lost touch with its grounding in the real world. Christians had forgotten that biblical religion is a historical religion, based in real political events in particular cultures in actual historical periods, what biblical scholars call salvation history. Moses was a historical figure. Jesus was a historical figure. Moses led the people of God out of a historical slavery, fed them through

God's help with real food (the manna in the desert), guided them to a physical land, and gave them a political future. Jesus actually lived, actually died, and actually rose again. These are not just spiritual archetypes, even if they are also spiritual archetypes.

Now this spiritualizing tendency of Christians is one that we can continue to observe today. If you keep your ears attuned you will notice it happening again and again. It is amazing the number of times that you will hear a historical story from the Bible given a contemporary spiritualized meaning.

If Moses leads the people out of the land of Egypt, then the message drawn is not that God wills historical, political freedom for today's imprisoned peoples – perhaps in Bosnia and Colombia, in Northern Ireland and Nigeria, in Haiti and indeed in Palestine. The message is often that Moses stands for the need to give your whole heart to God and find Jesus as your personal saviour.

If Jesus heals an illness the message drawn is not that we should share in his health-giving work through, for example, becoming doctors or promoting the National Health Service. The message drawn is that God heals the unseen maladies of the soul.

And if Mary, the mother of Jesus, in her *Magnificat* which we sing regularly at evensong, says that 'He hath filled the hungry with good things, and the rich he hath sent empty away', then the message drawn is not that God wills a redistribution of wealth. The message drawn is that this is beautiful poetry, not to mention beautiful music.

In the late 1960s, early 1970s, a new theological school began in Latin America which attempted to counterbalance this tendency. It is known as Liberation Theology, and its first great exponent was an indigenous priest from Peru called Gustavo Gutiérrez, who published a book in 1971 called *A Theology of Liberation*, which then gave its name to the movement. 'Biblical faith' he said, 'is, above all, faith in a God who reveals himself through historical events, a God who saves in history.' And 'The liberation from Egypt – both a historical fact and at the same time a fertile Biblical theme – enriches this vision and is moreover its true source' (*A Theology of Liberation*,

English translation published by Orbis, 1973, pp. 154–5). In this work, and in the work of all subsequent liberation theologians, the exodus claimed a special place as a paradigm of liberation.

To ears that had been doped with spiritualizing interpretations for centuries, the theology of liberation sounded a strange and discordant note. Here were people, calling themselves theologians, talking of poverty, oppression, liberation, even revolution. Many European theologians reacted at first with the accusation that the liberation theologians were distorting the Christian message in the opposite direction: that they were *reducing* the biblical message to a purely political dimension. And so there has been a certain tension over this development.

The 'Vatican Instruction on Certain Aspects of the Theology of Liberation', issued in 1984, recognized that 'the exodus, in fact, is the fundamental event in the formation of the chosen people', but it characterised the liberation as 'marked by the gift of God's Spirit and the conversion of hearts' (IV.3–4). Whereas, it claimed:

> the new hermeneutic inherent in the 'theologies of liberation' leads to an essentially political rereading of the scriptures. Thus a major importance is given to the exodus event inasmuch as it is a liberation from political servitude. Likewise a political reading of the *Magnificat* is proposed. The mistake here is not in bringing attention to a political dimension of the readings of scripture, but in making of this one dimension the principal or exclusive component. This leads to a reductionist reading of the Bible.

Here we had the critique of the liberation theologians turned on its head. They had criticized European theology for giving a principally or exclusively spiritualized, other-worldly reading of the Bible, which was reductionist. European theology was now coming back at them and accusing them of doing the opposite, of giving a principally or exclusively politicized, this-worldly reading of the Bible.

But note that both sides are agreed on the fundamental principle – both aspects are essential to the Christian message.

A Christianity robbed of its historical, this-worldly context is thoroughly unbiblical: if you are willing to lose the way in which God acts in history, forging his salvation through the liberation of those who are in any way imprisoned, then you are abandoning the Judeo-Christian tradition. At the same time a Christianity robbed of its dimension of the afterlife is one that has lost its resurrection faith and its faith in the ultimate victory of God's justice.

The liberation theologians were very hurt by the Vatican attack, because they believed, and I think they were right, that their position had been misrepresented. Gustavo Gutiérrez himself, in a new edition of his book *A Theology of Liberation*, inserted a new introduction, which made even clearer what he believed was already quite clear in the text. He said he always distinguished different 'levels or dimensions of liberation in Christ ... liberation from social structures of oppression and marginalisation that force many ... to live in conditions contrary to God's will for their life', and also 'a personal transformation by which we live with profound inner freedom in the face of every kind of servitude, and ... finally ... liberation from sin.'

'There is not the slightest tinge of immanentism in this approach to integral liberation,' he says. That is, integral liberation, liberation of the whole person, body and soul, now and hereafter, does not in the slightest way imply there is no soul, no transcendent, no afterlife. He continues, defending himself against his detractors, 'but if any expression I have used may have given the impression that there is, I want to say here as forcefully as I can that any interpretation along those lines is incompatible with my position.'

So much for the theoretical background to two very different theological approaches, with their opposite emphases and opposite temptations, though with their common agreed principles of the unity of body and soul, the kingdom of God both here among us and still to come. But, you may ask: what does all this say to me?

I will tell you what it says to you. I am not going to fix my beady eye upon you and say 'Are you saved?' But I may fix my beady eye upon you and say 'Are you working for liberation?

Are you conforming your aims with those of God, the great "I am who I am", in those words of fire from the burning bush: "I have observed the misery of my people ... I have heard their cry ... I know their sufferings, and I have come down to deliver them."'

Do we, do you, do I, observe the misery of God's people in this country and around the world? Do we hear their cry? Do we know their sufferings? Are we working to deliver them? Are we responding as Moses did to the invitation to help make God's kingdom come? Do we realize what we are saying every time we say that prayer: 'Our Father ... thy kingdom come, thy will be done on earth as it is in heaven'?

The liberation theologians always say that those who understand the Bible best are the poor, because the good news of liberation is written particularly for them. I leave you with the insight of a poor woman from a basic ecclesial community in Brazil into the very text we have read tonight. The biblical theologian, Carlos Mesters, tells the story:

> At one session we were reading the following text: 'I have heard the cries of my people' (Exodus 3.7). A woman who worked in a factory offered this commentary: 'The Bible does not say that God has heard the praying of the people. It says that God has heard the cries of his people. I don't mean that people shouldn't pray. I mean that people should imitate God. Very often we work to get people to go to church and pray first; and only then will we pay heed to their cries.' (John Eagleson and Sergio Torres (eds) *The Challenge of Basic Christian Communities*, Orbis, 1981, p. 207)

And, adds Mesters, 'you just won't find that sort of interpretation in books'.

Let us pray then tonight that our ears may be open to hear the muffled cries of the oppressed, that our eyes may be open to search out the forgotten and unseen ones, that our minds may be open to know the sorrows of all those who God loves, that our wills may be open to find ways of delivering them, and that our hearts may burn with the passionate and creative flames of God's justice.

CHAPTER SIX

First, Elijah Must Come

Malachi 3.1–6; 4; Hebrews 11.17 – 12.2

Today is the last Sunday of the year, before Advent begins. It is not often one gets a chance to speak about the very last words of the Old Testament, but tonight we have them:

> Lo, I will send you the prophet Elijah before the great and terrible day of the Lord comes. He will turn the hearts of parents to their children and the hearts of children to their parents, so that I will not come and strike the land with a curse. (Malachi 4.5–6)

The fascinating question I want to explore with you tonight is this: who is this Elijah the prophet?

Of course we recognize that we are hearing prophecies of the coming of the Messiah. The text from that first reading from Malachi begins 'See, I am sending my messenger to prepare the way before me.' The verse is familiar to us because we hear it repeated at the very beginning of Mark's gospel:

> The beginning of the good news of Jesus Christ, the Son of God. As it is written in the prophet Isaiah, 'See, I am sending my messenger ahead of you, who will prepare your way'. (Mark 1.1–2)

Only Mark got the reference wrong: it is not Isaiah but Malachi.

So the Old Testament ends as Mark's gospel begins – and Mark is generally accepted to be the first of the gospels. Now there does not seem to be much doubt in Mark's mind about who Elijah was. He continues:

The voice of one crying out in the wilderness:
    'Prepare the way of the Lord,
    make his paths straight',
John the baptizer appeared in the wilderness, proclaiming
a baptism of repentance. (Mark 1.3–4)

Elijah, according to Mark, is clearly John the Baptist, about
whom we shall hear a lot in Advent.

And not just according to Mark. Luke shares the same view.
John's father, Zechariah, is told that his son will go before the
Lord their God 'with the spirit and power of Elijah' (Luke
1.17). And Jesus himself confirms the identification of John the
Baptist with the forerunner Elijah figure in Luke 7.24–7,
quoting from the same text of Malachi:

This is the one about whom it is written,
    'See, I am sending my messenger ahead of you,
    who will prepare your way before you.'

And Matthew, in a parallel text, has Jesus say just the same
(Matthew 11.10). And he makes it even clearer in chapter 17
when Jesus tells the disciples:

Elijah has already come, and they did not recognize him,
but they did to him whatever they pleased .... Then the
disciples understood that he was speaking to them about
John the Baptist. (Matthew 17.12–13)

So 'Who is Elijah?' looks like an easy question. Or is it quite so
simple? When we come to the fourth gospel, we find a different
answer. When the priests and Levites came from Jerusalem to
ask John, 'Who are you?' they ask him specifically, 'Are you
Elijah?' to which he says 'I am not' (John 1.21). 'Are you
Elijah?' was not just a silly arbitrary question: they all knew
their Malachi, and knew that Elijah was to be the forerunner
of the Christ.

Who then is Elijah, for the writer of the fourth gospel? One
theory of biblical scholars is that Elijah was Jesus himself. In
this first chapter, John the Baptist has denied, in turn, being
Messiah, Elijah and the prophet (John 1.20–1), but the person
to whom these three titles really point is Jesus himself. (This

idea is explained, with a reconstruction of an earlier version of the text, in John Ashton's book *Understanding the Fourth Gospel*, Clarendon Press, 1991, pp. 252–6.)

There are at least two other suggestions that can be made to furnish an answer to the question 'Who is Elijah?' If we recall the Transfiguration story, which is told by Matthew, Mark and Luke, then we remember that on the top of the mountain where Jesus had gone to pray he is seen in the company of Moses and Elijah. Elijah does indeed come at this point, before the crucial cycle of salvation, and is seen by the three disciples, Peter, James and John.

Another suggestion, that I make in my book *Six New Gospels: New Testament Women Tell Their Stories* (Geoffrey Chapman, 1994), is that the woman who anoints Jesus at Bethany is Elijah. Why? Because one of the key acts of Elijah is to anoint. In the revelation of God given to Elijah in the 'still small voice' on Mount Horeb he is authorized to anoint Hazael and Jehu as kings, and Elisha as prophet (1 Kings 19.15–16).

Again, in Ecclesiasticus 48.8 Elijah is characterized as one who anointed kings and prophets. The woman who anoints Jesus at Bethany shares in this action of Elijah – anointing the one who is to be king, anointing the one who is to be prophet. Once this prophetic action of anointing has taken place, the final tragic action of redemption is ready to unroll: Elijah has come, and within a week of this decisive anointing, Jesus will be dead – and risen.

Or, of course, it can be said that Elijah never came, and that therefore Jesus was not the Messiah, was not the one for whom Elijah paved the way. And that was the response of some at the cross, who misheard Jesus' dying cry *'Eli, Eli, lema sabachthani'* and said 'Listen, he is calling for Elijah . . . let us see whether Elijah will come to take him down' (Mark 15.35–6, cf. Matthew 27.46–7). Elijah did not come, proving, they thought, that Jesus was not the Messiah.

But why does Elijah matter? And what does he mean for us? I often say that we have to become adopted Jews to enter into an understanding of who Jesus is. But it is still difficult to take on board a tradition that is not familiar. It is hard for us to find a meaning in the Elijah tradition. We may find it easier to believe Jesus is the Christ, than to believe that John the Baptist, or any of the other candidates, is Elijah, or that Elijah plays any role at all. How then, can we make sense of this Elijah figure for ourselves today?

Perhaps the question should not be 'Who is Elijah?', with that assumption of objective truth, but the more subjective question 'Who is Elijah for me?' 'Who, for me, is the one who points the way to Christ?' And then the question becomes much easier. For all of us who have come to know Christ, there has been someone who has pointed the way. Perhaps a friend, perhaps a teacher, perhaps a priest, perhaps a great preacher or evangelist, perhaps someone we have never met like Nelson Mandela or Mother Teresa or the Salvadorean martyr Archbishop Oscar Romero, who have stirred hundreds and thousands to a faith and a hope. Perhaps someone who is still influential in our lives. Or perhaps someone whose role, like John the Baptist, was to decrease as Christ increased for us – someone we grew out of and moved away from, or someone who we will grow out of and move away from. Whoever it is, there is almost certainly somebody who led us and inspired us, whose words made our hearts burn within us, who pointed to Jesus for us. Someone who for each one of us stands in the tradition of those wonderful Old Testament men and women listed in our second reading from Hebrews 11: Abraham, Isaac, Jacob, Moses, Rahab, Gideon and Barak, Samson and Jephthah, David and Samuel and the prophets.

Recognizing the Elijah figure or figures for each of us means recognizing that we are people who need other people if we are to come to faith. It means recognizing our interdependence – that we are a body of Christ, a communion of sinners who need one another. God's grace is supreme, but it is mediated to us through other people.

Recognizing the Elijah figure or figures also means recognizing that the forerunner must pass away. We are, in the words of Hebrews, surrounded by a 'cloud of witnesses'. We remember them, we thank them, we owe them our gratitude for the rest of our lives, and yet – as at the transfiguration – we let the cloud of witnesses pass, to reveal the brightness and the glory of one person alone.

His words will never pass, nor his ideas become stale. We shall never grow out of him. All our lives let us grow into him. When we remember the Elijahs in our lives, we remember that the entire point of a forerunner is to be a forerunner, to whet our palate for the one who is to come. The one who is to come – whose coming we will wait for and long for throughout Advent – is whole and complete and perfect and worthy of all our adoration. In the words of Hebrews he is 'the pioneer and perfecter of our faith' (Hebrews 12.2). In the words of Malachi he is 'the sun of righteousness' which will rise 'with healing in its wings' (Malachi 4.2).

CHAPTER SEVEN

Strangers in the Land of Egypt

Deuteronomy 10.12 – 11.1; Revelation 3.7–22

> You shall also love the stranger, for you were strangers in the land of Egypt. (Deuteronomy 10.19)

Two local events come to mind concerned with the welcome or lack of welcome that we give to the stranger. One was a day conference on black theology, which spoke of the influences on British black theology of Asian theology, African theology and North American theology. The final black speaker, Ron Nathan, concluded powerfully (with certain overtones about the lack of welcome and collaboration his people experience): 'We are prepared to make our contribution to the evangelization of the UK. We will do it as partners. Or else we will do it alone.'

The other event was a series of simultaneous demonstrations all over the country outside prisons and other centres where asylum-seekers are currently held. Locally we had a demonstration outside Campsfield House immigration detention centre, and some forty people were there, including students. These demonstrators are asking for an end to the detention of asylum-seekers, whether in the grim conditions of large Victorian jails alongside hardened criminals, or even in the more comfortable conditions of specially furnished detention centres.

Concern over this issue led the Catholic bishops' conference of England and Wales to publish a statement saying:

> If detained, asylum seekers become ... unconvicted and

unsentenced prisoners. Confinement and isolation, with the trauma of having just fled the threat of persecution, causes acute psychological stress. Many detainees are reported to be clinically depressed, inflict self-injury or attempt suicide .... The human cost of detention is too high and the government should consider alternative measures.

But I do not wish to give you a particular political line on this, partly because that is not the task of a preacher, and partly because I do not in any case know what I think. Those opposed to detention say that it is wrong to detain an asylum-seeker unless there are very exceptional circumstances; they say it is a false judgement that such people are liable to abscond – they do not. For their part, the Home Office say they only detain people under the Immigration Act when there *are* very exceptional circumstances. Out of 47,000 asylum applications awaiting a decision (at the time of preparing this address), just 640 individuals are in detention, less than one and a half per cent. The Home Office maintain detention is not the normal way they treat those seeking asylum, but rather the way that is required in unusual circumstances where there is reason to believe that people will abscond. Against this, many visitors to detention centres say this picture just does not fit the people they meet.

I do not intend to make a judgement on whether or not the detention centres should be closed down. The invitation of the scriptures is to form our attitude before such cases, rather than to determine what are the best political means to achieve the ends we are looking for. And the attitude is this: 'You shall also love the stranger, for you were strangers in the land of Egypt.' Well, we may not have been, but we can imagine what it would be like if we were. We can open our ears to hear what one refugee woman said when she saw some graffiti that said 'Refugee go home'. 'Don't they understand', she said, 'I *want* to go home.'

The second reading can lead us into a further insight on the idea of welcoming the stranger. 'Listen! I am standing at the door, knocking.' I cannot hear those words without being reminded of the painting by William Holman Hunt, one copy of which is in St Paul's Cathedral and the other in Keble College chapel, Oxford. It is worth seeing these original works and not just a postcard reproduction.

In a reproduction we may be struck by how unfortunately Anglo-Saxon the figure of Christ is, a classic fair-skinned hero, all rather pretty and not a good model for the stranger who represents something different from our life. But if we go to look at the painting itself, we see it is all much darker than on the postcard.

Holman Hunt has painted a night visit by an unknown stranger. The door, which has no external handle, is overgrown with weeds and a sinister dark green glow enshrouds everything with the danger of the unknown. The painting evokes all the sense of fear that people feel when, at some unpredictable hour in the middle of the night, there is a knock on the door, and there is no peephole to check out the identity of the visitor.

The drama of the portrayal is that out of a situation which is dark and frightening and unknown, there is in fact a shining promise awaiting us. Christ carries a lantern, as the light of the world; his halo also shines and his cloak is jewelled. If we take the risk of opening to the unknown stranger, even in a moment of darkness and fear, then we may be rewarded by finding we have opened to someone so precious that we would never dream of keeping him out if we had first seen what was on offer. And so the translation of the NRSV makes good sense: not the somewhat static and formal 'Behold I stand at the door and knock' that may be more familiar to us, but something happening this very moment. 'Listen! I am standing at the door, knocking; if you hear my voice and open the door, I will come in to you and eat with you, and you with me' (Revelation 3.20).

When we apply this to refugees we are taken a stage beyond the Old Testament text, 'You shall also love the stranger, for you were strangers in the land of Egypt.' That gives us one kind of motivation for offering a welcome – kindness and gratitude and a sense of putting ourselves in others' shoes. The New Testament gives us a further motivation: when we open the door to strangers we find we are opening to Christ.

We may remember also Jesus' words, 'I was a stranger and you welcomed me' (Matthew 25.35). And again in Matthew, Jesus becomes the refugee who goes to Egypt. He flees, as a baby, for his life, becoming himself the stranger in Egypt, as his ancestors had been before him. And so Jesus' identification with the refugee becomes total, and the asylum-seeker of today represents Jesus to us in a very intimate way. The benefit is to us, not just to them.

This transition is a crucial one – from feeling that we are the ones being kind, to realizing that we are the ones to benefit. Opening the door to Christ cannot be simplistically translated into a completely undiscriminating open-door policy on immigration, but it can be the foundation for making difficult policy decisions inspired by an attitude of welcoming and valuing the dark stranger on the other side of the door. Those involved in the campaign to close detention centres for immigrants are surely driven by this instinct, and they believe it is not an attitude shared by the government.

Similarly the conference on black theology was not to urge us to be kind to black theologians, nor to show us how the black people are coming along nicely and catching up with the white people in their theology. It was to show how white theology can be enriched by the thought and experiences of the different black theologies, which offer insights we would never reach on our own. The insights of black theology are like the jewels glowing on the cloak of Christ the stranger – the dark figure on the other side of the door, who knocks on the door not just so that he can find shelter, but also so that we can have the joy of eating with him.

Along these lines I would like to end by reading to you a famous and moving passage from a document of the Jesuit Refugee Service, meeting in Thailand in 1985. The nine regional co-ordinators, coming from refugee areas all around the world, said this:

> We want to place special emphasis on being with rather than doing for. We want our presence among refugees to be one of sharing with them, of accompaniment, of walking together along the same path. In so far as

possible, we want to feel what they have felt, suffer as they have, share the same hopes and aspirations, see the world through their eyes. We ourselves would like to become one with the poor and oppressed peoples so that, all together, we can begin the search for a new life.

This attempt to identify with the poor and rejected, however hesitant and imperfect, has brought us untold blessings. For by their very poverty they teach us to become detached from material possessions and our own selves. Their insecurity and uncertainty about the future show us how not to rely merely on ourselves or on human planning. Their cultural values and simple dignity as human beings remind us that a person's worth is determined by what he is rather than by what he has. Their openness and generosity so often challenge us to share with them and others all that we have and are. Their happiness and laughter in the midst of adversity help us to understand the true meaning of suffering. Their deep faith and unfailing hope lead us to rediscover these spiritual values in our own lives. In a word, we have found Christ again in the faces and lives of these abandoned people, a Christ who is beckoning and calling us to follow him. (From a statement by the Jesuit Refugee Service, 21 November 1985; The Seven Fountains, Chiang Mai, Thailand)

CHAPTER EIGHT

Advent Sunday

Isaiah 40.1–11; Luke 1.26–38

Today is the last Sunday of term, and the first day of Advent.
Observing Advent is not the same as celebrating Christmas in
advance. Advent means 'coming, approaching'. Christ is
expected, he has not yet arrived.

Advent is the pregnancy period of our faith. So we listen to
Luke's story of the annunciation, when Mary hears that she is
expecting a baby. Pregnancy is a time for abstaining from
indulgence, for giving up smoking and alcohol and late nights.
So too Advent is a time when people give up luxuries, as they do
in Lent. It is a time for creating the best possible conditions for
the new life to come.

Advent is the time of preparing the way of the Lord. So we
hear also Isaiah's prophecy about the voice in the wilderness,
which reaches its fulfilment in John the Baptist's call to
repentance.

And just as John called the people to repentance, so too that
was the burning message that Jesus taught. From the first
moment that he began to preach, he said, 'Repent, and believe
in the good news' (Mark 1.15). In Matthew's parallel text, the
words are practically the same: 'Repent, for the reign of heaven
has come near' (Matthew 4.17).

'Repent' is not a word that we much like these days, but it
reminds us of the foundational Christian teaching that what is
wrong with the world is sin. The truth is not that everyone else
except me is to blame, but that I too am a sinner. And the way
to put things right is through salvation from sin – forgiveness of
the past, healing for the future. Us forgiving others. God

forgiving us. And us accepting with joy and huge relief the good news that we don't have to go on justifying ourselves, because it is OK to say: 'I was wrong, I am sorry'.

If this is Jesus' opening message in Matthew and Mark, what are his first words in Luke and John? In two entirely different contexts he says surprisingly similar things: 'Why were you searching for me?' (Luke 2.49) and 'What are you looking for?' (John 1.38). The disciples in John were of course looking for Jesus, just as Mary and Joseph were looking for Jesus when they lost him, aged twelve, in Luke's account.

So we have the foundational gospel message expressed through another image – that of searching. Searching is a concept more congenial to modern culture than the language of repentance, though there is no conflict in the substance of the message.

We are searchers, and it is good to be searchers, and we should search persistently, passionately, tirelessly. When we find Jesus we will know that we have found what we are looking for, and we will want to remain with him. As Mary and Joseph did in Nazareth. As the two disciples at the beginning of John's gospel did when they went home with Jesus that day. Again this is a message of joy and huge relief. It is good news.

In an Advent service we hear again and again repeated the Advent cries for Christ, 'O come, O come.' Usually we focus rather on the call by Jesus, 'come and follow me'; but loving is a two-way business and the call is now the other way round.

> O Wisdom, come.
> O King of the Nations, come.
> O root of Jesse, come.
> O Emmanuel, come.
> O dayspring, come.
> O key of David, come.
> O Adonai, come.

These words are reminiscent of the words on the last page of the Bible: ' "I am coming soon." Amen. Come, Lord Jesus' (Revelation 22.20).

The plaintive and persistent cry for the coming of God makes

Advent what it is. And today's world has given us plenty of cause for that. To take just three quotes from this week's media:

> Britain's aid to the poor of the Third World will now be slashed by £150 million.

> A young man who shot dead his common-law wife in a car-park had been granted bail by magistrates on a domestic violence offence despite police fears for his wife's safety.

> I went back to Rwanda again and saw the victims ... a whole nation with its soul hacked to pieces.

Add to that our varied sorts of personal mess, and a plaintive and persistent cry 'O come' is exactly what is needed in this crooked and desperate world.

I have a friend who says that Advent is his favourite season. Why? I think because Advent is a time of exquisite balance between the sadness of the mess we live in, and the bliss of the world we would like to live in. Advent is when we acknowledge that bliss is not the blotting out of pain with port and plum pudding, but a process, a pilgrimage, a pregnancy, and – amidst the chaos of the world's governing – a cry for the coming of the reign of God.

DEEPENING FAITH

CHAPTER NINE

Crossing the Abyss of Death

Deuteronomy 8.1–10; John 6.1–21

Some of you will know, some of you will not know, that since I last spoke to you I have been bereaved. Every time I have addressed you I have been in a position of bearing witness to faith. But death, particularly the death of someone as close as a husband, is when faith is really tested, when faith really counts. As St Paul says: 'If there is no resurrection of the dead . . . then our proclamation has been in vain and your faith has been in vain' (1 Corinthians 15.13). I want then to come before you today and say, yes I believe our faith is not in vain, yes I believe in the resurrection of the dead.

Having a Christian faith does in fact make an enormous difference to how we react to death. Less than twenty-four hours before my husband died, his doctor came to our house and told him that he was going to get better slowly. When I asked this same doctor afterwards how surprised he was to hear of the death he replied, 'Not very surprised at all.' But, he explained, the last thing he thought you should say to someone in danger of death was that their life was in danger, for it would increase anxiety and hasten the end. Exactly the same was told to the family of one of my son's friends, as the father lay in an Italian hospital riddled with cancer: don't tell him, it would kill him.

I know someone who worked in a geriatric hospital who found that clergy visits to the dying were not encouraged, because they frightened the other patients. When my own pious

Catholic mother-in-law died in hospital we asked the nurses if they had called the priest before her death. 'No', they replied. 'Why not?' 'Well', they said, 'you see it was so sudden.' But she had been in the hospital for a week, awaiting death.

This avoidance of the issue of death is an attitude which is diametrically opposite to the old Christian tradition of preparing for death. You would confess your sins and receive the food for your journey in the last sacraments; you would be anointed. There was even a tradition of preparing for death through every moment of life. A Catholic child used to be taught in the Penny Catechism to go to bed every night prepared lest death strike unexpectedly. 'I should ... occupy myself with the thoughts of death; and endeavour to compose myself to rest at the foot of the cross, and give my last thoughts to my crucified Saviour' (A.370).

In the Christian tradition death is not the undoing of life, the opposite of life, but the climax of life, the point of our existence, the final examination to which everything up till then has been leading. Just as it would be cruel beyond excuse to fail to tell a student the date of her examinations, so it would be nonsensical to withhold from a patient the proximity of his death, depriving him of the right to prepare for the most serious examination of his life.

I do not say this because I want to complain about the medical profession today, who may not be adequately trained in dealing with those they cannot heal, but who always behave with the greatest concern and most generous and conscientious care. I say it simply because I want to point up the contrast between two radically opposing attitudes to death: death as the end of life, and death as the beginning of eternal life.

By pure coincidence, the two readings from today's lectionary are extraordinarily close to those we chose for my husband's funeral. So you will understand it is difficult for me to read them without seeing what I saw at our requiem. But I know that I will not be the only one here to have been in close contact with death. Probably most of you, perhaps all of you, will have your own experiences – if not of a spouse, then of a parent, or a grandparent. Death is a concern that touches us all, and I hope my reflections will be of relevance to all.

The first reading speaks of the time of homeless wandering before the entry into the promised land. This reading speaks of the old Jerusalem, while our funeral reading (Revelation 21) spoke of the new Jerusalem. In both cases there is a time of wandering, a time of testing and of waiting, when hope is sustained by the promise of what is to come.

The old Jerusalem will be:

> a good land, a land with flowing streams, with springs and underground waters welling up in valleys and hills, a land of wheat and barley, of vines and fig trees and pomegranates, a land of olive trees and honey, a land where you may eat bread without scarcity, where you will lack nothing. (Deuteronomy 8.7–9)

The new Jerusalem will be a land where God 'will wipe every tear from their eyes', and 'death will be no more; mourning and crying and pain will be no more'.

The image of homelessness is evoked in the ancient *Salve Regina* prayer addressed to Christ's mother: 'After this our exile, show unto us the fruit of thy womb Jesus'. The time of exile is our time on this earth, but the specific time of wandering in the desert after the release from Egyptian bondage may fittingly be seen as the time of purgatory or purgation. This is the time when those who have made a basic choice for good and for God are purged of what still remains in them of sin, so that the face of God may shine fully before them. This is what is called the Beatific Vision, and there are few who die so pure that we believe nothing at all remains between them and God.

The idea of purgatory also frees Christian faith from the charge of being facile consolation, a nice idea to hang on to in the face of the ultimate absurdity of death. After death there is something more to say beyond 'and he lived happily ever after'. Death is tough not soft, it is about facing the truth not evading it, about reality not illusion, about justice not whitewash. The judgement of God frightens us – *dies irae, dies illa* (on that day, that day of wrath), in the opening words of the famous sequence from the mass for the dead – just as also the pain of dying frightens us.

But the consolation of Christian faith comes only through

taking us through these awful realities, not by bypassing them and pretending they do not exist. Heaven is only heaven for lying on the other side of purgatory, just as the promised land of milk and honey is only a land of promise for lying on the other side of the wilderness.

Purgatory, then, should not be seen as a severe notion, but rather as a tremendously compassionate idea. It permits us and those we love to move closer to God even after the moment of death. It allows the fundamental option of a life to be strengthened and purified, rid of all that spoils it. That is why, in the *Dream of Gerontius*, written by John Henry Newman and set to music by Elgar, the dying man cries out spontaneously, of his own free choice – as his eyes are fully opened to God's truth:

> Take me away, and in the lowest deep
>   There let me be,
> And there in hope the long night-watches keep,
>   Told out for me.
> There motionless and happy in my pain,
>   Lone, not forlorn –
> There will I sing my sad perpetual strain,
>   Until the morn,
> There will I sing and soothe my stricken breast,
>   Which ne'er can cease
> To throb, and pine, and languish, till possest
>   Of its Sole Peace.
> There will I sing my absent Lord and Love:
>   Take me away.
> That sooner I may rise, and go above,
>   And see Him in the truth of everlasting day.

'The lowest deep ...', 'the long night-watches keep ....' The theme of night and the deep brings us to today's gospel reading, as Jesus walks on the water in the night.

In ancient Hebrew thought, the deeps of the sea represented the forces of evil and chaos, which God divided in the act of creation at the beginning of Genesis. The Psalmist cries:

> Save me, O God,
> for the waters have come up to my neck ...

> Do not let the flood sweep over me,
> or the deep swallow me up,
> or the Pit close its mouth over me. (Psalm 69.1, 15)

And again:

> When the waters saw you, O God,
> when the waters saw you, they were afraid;
> the very deep trembled. (Psalm 77.16)

God is the one who 'trampled the waves of the Sea' (Job 9.8).

And so when the disciples saw Jesus walking on the water, and were afraid, they felt themselves to be in the presence of God in the primeval battle against evil. And they put this into words in the story of the calming of the storm, which is a story from the synoptic gospels that relates closely to the walking on the water: 'Who then is this, that even the wind and the sea obey him?' (Mark 4.41) they ask in awe. The unspoken answer is: 'It is God'.

This answer becomes even more heavily implied in the reading from John today, because Jesus says to the frightened disciples, 'It is I', in Greek, literally 'I am'. This is a reference back to God's famous words of self-revelation to Moses from the burning bush: 'I AM WHO I AM. . . . Thus you shall say to the Israelites, "I AM has sent me to you" ' (Exodus 3.14).

When Jesus walks on the water, he is not just doing a bit of 'geewizzery'. His miracle bears profound symbolic significance, not just of his power over the laws of nature but of his power over evil, of his power over death.

In Matthew's parallel to today's gospel (Matthew 14.22–33), there is a further detail to the story. When Jesus speaks to them and says, 'It is I [or I am]; do not be afraid', Peter, who is in the boat, replies:

> 'Lord, if it is you, command me to come to you on the water'. He said, 'Come.' So Peter got out of the boat, started walking on the water and came towards Jesus. But when he noticed the strong wind he became frightened and beginning to sink, he cried out, 'Lord, save me.' Jesus immediately reached out his hand and caught him saying to him 'You of little faith, why did you doubt?' When they got in the boat,

the wind ceased. And those in the boat worshipped him, saying, 'Truly you are the Son of God'. (Matthew 14.28–33)

Because my husband was called Peter, this was the gospel we chose for his funeral, and this was the text we wrote on his memorial card: 'Peter answered him, "Lord, if it is you, command me to come to you on the water." He said, "come".'

We fear, we all fear, crossing the waters of death, because the depths are hidden and menacing. Yet the death rate remains what it has always been: one hundred per cent. The gospel gives us a vivid image of crossing that abyss, with faith, or with less faith, with 'little faith', when we are still caught by the hand and borne up.

We all fear death, and few there are who say yes to it when they have the choice – we call them martyrs. But here we are given an image to give us courage, the image of Christ calling us to himself, the one who crossed death and rose again, the one in whose resurrection we place our faith. He will sustain us on that journey of fear. And at the end of it we shall find ourselves in his arms.

CHAPTER TEN

On Not Confusing
God's Call

1 Samuel 3.1 – 4.1a; John 1.35–51

We are in the week of prayer for Christian unity, which is a time for remembering how easily we follow the call of religious leaders in place of following the call of God. And confusion over a call happens to be just what today's first reading is about. God calls Samuel, and he confuses the source of the voice, thinking it comes from the priest Eli.

It is not always easy to tell the difference between the call of God and the call of someone else. It is not so difficult to discern between something quite good and something quite bad – between, say, greed and self-sacrifice: they just feel completely different, arousing quite different responses in us. The problem comes when we try to discern between the pure essence of God's call and the way God's call reaches us, mediated by other people and interpreted by the fallibility of our own minds. That is where we often make a confusion, and sometimes there are hard and bitter battles, with both sides claiming God is on their side. So it was at the Reformation, from which we have still not recovered. So it is today – over, for instance, the ordination of women.

I have keen memories of being present in the cathedral for the diocese of Monmouth, seeing eight new women priests ordained for the Church in Wales, and Bishop Rowan Williams quoted the words of T. S. Eliot:

> A cold coming we had of it,
> Just the worst time of the year

> For a journey, and such a long journey
> ... this Birth was
> Hard and bitter agony for us, like Death.

How sad it is that the churches – the Church of England, the Anglican Church in Wales, the Roman Catholic Church, and others – should be torn apart internally in such a hard and bitter agony on this issue, with one side claiming it is sticking fast to the call of God, resisting change, and the other side insisting it is following the call of God, into God's future.

How often it happens that people believe they are following God's call, and later find they are mistaken. This can happen even when people have some kind of a vision or revelation, with a sense of absolute certainty that God is telling them something – the sort of gratuitous experience that St Ignatius of Loyola described as 'consolation without preceding cause'. I remember hearing of a childless couple who, after years of waiting, finally had an operation to improve their fertility, and one evening shortly afterwards they had a mystical experience: they felt they knew, just knew, that they would have a child – perhaps rather as God promised a son to Abraham. But the irony is, they never did.

What then do we make of the God-given sense of certainty? St Ignatius' answer was that we can have a genuine revelation from God that leaves no room for doubt, and yet misinterpretation can creep in as we interpret its meaning. He writes:

> When the consolation is without cause, even though there is no deception in it, as it comes from God Our Lord alone, as has been said, nevertheless the spiritual person to whom God gives this consolation must scrutinise the experience carefully and attentively, so as to distinguish the exact time of the actual consolation from the period following it, during which the soul is still aglow and favoured with the after-effects of the consolation now passed. For during this second period it often happens, owing either to thinking based on conclusions drawn from the relations between our own concepts and judgements, or to the agency of the good or bad spirit, that we form

various plans and opinions that are not directly given to us by God Our Lord. These therefore require to be examined with very great care before being given complete credence and put into practice. (*Spiritual Exercises*, 336, in *Saint Ignatius of Loyola: Personal Writings*, trans. Joseph A. Munitiz and Philip Endean, Penguin Classics, 1996)

This explains how, with the best will in the world, Christians can sometimes be locked in fierce controversy with each other, with both sides feeling they have a call from God, which they cannot refuse to follow: Protestants against Catholics, opponents of women priests against their supporters.

I can never hear the reading of the call of Samuel without remembering the moving way Sheila Cassidy wrote about it in her book *Audacity to Believe*. Sheila Cassidy, who used to be a student at Oxford, went to work in Chile as a doctor in 1971. She became involved in tending someone who was sought by the police, and was tortured for information. Shortly before this happened she made a retreat, according to the Ignatian Spiritual Exercises, and it was this text of 1 Samuel that became crucial to her in her spiritual struggle to give an unconditional Yes to God. She wrote:

My day was largely spent in prayer and I spoke to no one except my guide, who came in the afternoon to see how I was progressing. Much of the time I spent in the garden praying on top of a pile of fallen leaves. It made an excellent couch, being soft and dry, and the leaves lying on the ground around me made a loud noise if anyone walked on them so I had no fear of being surprised in this undignified position. I ate my meals alone and in silence, and my life at the hospital and at home seemed a thousand miles away as I faced myself and my maker in the quiet of the retreat house garden. With no one to talk to and no novels to read there was no escaping, and I ceased running and tried to listen to what God had to say to me.

After five days of prayer and reflection I was asked to read and meditate upon a passage from the third chapter of the book of Samuel. I read that the Lord called Samuel three times and that the boy did not understand who was calling until he was told by his master to go and lie down and that if the Lord called, he was to say, 'Speak, Lord, for your servant hears.' So it was that on a winter morning in 1975 I lay face down on a pile of leaves at the bottom of the garden in a Chilean retreat house and made those words of Samuel my own. As in the days of my childhood twenty years before I heard no voices and I saw no visions, but gradually it became clear to me that God was calling. I knew beyond any reasonable doubt that I was being asked to follow Him, for better or for worse, for richer or for poorer, in sickness or in health, for the rest of my life.

How can one convey the agony and the ecstasy of being called by God? At one moment one is overawed by the immensity of the honour, the incredible fact of having been chosen, and in the same breath one screams, 'No! No! Please, not me, I can't take it!' That which seconds ago was a privilege becomes an outrageously unfair demand. Why should I be the one asked to give up marriage and career? Why me? Why may I not lie with a man I love and bear his children? I have only one life; how can you ask me to sign it away as if it meant nothing to me? . . .

As I lay there in tears, my ears and my hair full of autumn leaves, I knew that this was the end of the chase. I had chosen to come to this place and I had invited God to speak and he had. Of course I was quite free to say, 'No, I don't want to'. But this would be a clear and deliberate refusal. I thought about it, and I knew that I did not want to say No and that, however much it hurt, I could only humbly accept. So, as hundreds of men and women had done before me, I said my 'Fiat'. (Sheila Cassidy, *Audacity to Believe*, pp. 122–3, Collins, 1977)

Sheila Cassidy returned to Britain, after her release from prison in Chile, convinced that she was called to become a nun. Yet she had confused the way God was calling her, and after trying her vocation in a convent she returned to medical practice.

Instead of a nun, she became instead one of the leading lights of the hospice movement, running a hospice in Plymouth. Yes, God was calling her. Yes, God was calling her to give over everything that she had and everything that she was. But no, God was not calling her to do that through being a nun. She heard the call, but she mistook the details.

The second reading tonight was about the call of the first disciples, according to John's gospel, where some of John the Baptist's disciples leave him to follow the one he has pointed out as the Lamb of God. In this octave of prayer for Christian unity it reminds us that it is not John the Baptist, or any other disciple or apostle whom we follow, but only the Christ. We do not belong (as we are reminded in 1 Corinthians) to Paul, nor to Apollos, nor to Peter. 'Has Christ been divided? Was Paul crucified for you? Or were you baptized in the name of Paul?' (1 Corinthians 1.13).

No, there is only one we should follow – Christ. Only one whose call must be followed – God. And Christ and God are one.

I leave you with a devotional suggestion. In that story of the call from John's gospel, we are given the names of all the disciples mentioned in the story, but one. There is Nathaniel, and Philip, and Simon Peter, and before them Andrew. 'One of the two who heard John speak and followed him was Andrew, Simon Peter's brother' (John 1.40). One of the two, but who was the other one? We are never told. Andrew's companion could have been an apostle, or not an apostle. It could have been a man or a woman.

You may, if you wish, imagine yourself in that place, yourself as one of the two who followed Jesus, saying 'Rabbi, where are you staying?' Why should that disciple not be you, in your prayerful imagination? You can put yourself in the story, as one of the two who heard the call 'Come and see', and went with Jesus, at about four o'clock in the afternoon, and stayed with him. Jesus' call to us is always there: to spend time with him, to get to know him, to live with him, to be influenced by his values, and to be shaped more and more as a follower of Christ.

With that thought in mind, may we all pray in this octave to discern the true call of God, to aspire to follow none but Jesus, and so to build the unity of his church. The church rests on only one foundation, on Jesus Christ our Lord.

CHAPTER ELEVEN

The Sower

Daniel 6; Matthew 13.1–9, 18–23

Tonight I want to speak about the growing period of the faith, as Jesus spoke of it in his parable of the sower. Let us recap on the parable.

There are four places where the seed falls. On the path, in shallow soil, on land contaminated with thorns, and in good earth. I think we all know people who correspond to each of the four categories.

First there is the seed on the path, that the birds came and ate up. These are people for whom the word goes in one ear and out the other; it just makes no impact, it is immediately forgotten.

This is like me when my son is trying to explain to me the details of the fantasy football league in which he is a keen (and talented) player, at present lying in second place. I must have asked him to explain the scoring method at least four times, but I have always forgotten the answer. Perhaps there have been times in our life when we have been like this with the gospel, when we perhaps were just not ready to be receptive. Our mind is on something else, and the good news goes to the birds.

Secondly there is the rocky ground, with little earth, where the seed springs up quickly but doesn't last; it withers for lack of soil. Here is the keen young convert. How do we know which converts will last and which fade away? Only time can tell.

When I was a keen young convert my teachers were convinced I would be a shallow-soil Christian who would not last, because I had been a difficult girl at convent school. Well, thirty years later I'm still hanging on. Another keen young convert I remember from those days of my youth was a schoolfriend of my brother, who afterwards became a distinguished novelist. He was very pious at the age of seventeen, and his faith impressed me, but he didn't last as a convert. Then there was a schoolfriend of mine who came with me to a Billy Graham meeting and 'went up', clammily clutching my hand for solidarity. She didn't last either. She has become a high-quality musician. These people have done some wonderful artistic things with their lives, things that are very pleasing to God, but they have not lasted in the faith. That is not a judgement, it is just a fact. Most of us know people who have shot up and fallen away.

Thirdly there is the soil contaminated with thorns, so that the cares of the world and the lure of wealth choke the faith. This does not usually happen to students. It is the sort of thing that happens to older Christians.

It can often be observed. As they become more successful they sometimes grow quite literally fatter, and what was a lively committed faith is blunted as they grow self-satisfied or clever-clever. I can think of quite prominent Christians who have developed quite unpleasant combative sides to their personalities as their sharp minds and flowing words have become sharper and more flowing. Speaking as a journalist I have to acknowledge that this is a particular danger for those of my profession. The faith may be there as before, but it gets entangled with weeds and thorns which spoil it. And conversely, it sometimes happens that people whose business ventures go wrong become nicer people in the process, their hard edges knocked off by worldly failure, their self-congratulation softened into solidarity with the unsuccessful.

Then there is the good soil which yields thirtyfold, or sixtyfold, or a hundredfold. That is what we want to be – good soil. The word of God is the seed. You are the soil, black and rich, warm and fertile, ready to produce green shoots, golden grain, colourful fruits. Those who are poised on the verge of their future working lives, with so many opportunities open and so many years ahead, will want to prepare themselves to be a fitting vessel for God's grace, to let the seed thrust down long and deep roots that will endure and hold you firm through the years ahead. And maybe those long roots have already grown, for even those of student age have many years behind them as well as many ahead.

Because the student years are a threshold period, a time both of youth and of maturity, they are an excellent time for thinking about being confirmed, for those who have not already taken that step. And for those who have, the student years are an excellent time for thinking more about what confirmation means. Confirmation is an important part of composting the earth. The baptism of a baby is like a sower scattering seed. No seed, no growth. For some, their Christian initiation will come to absolutely nothing, like seed on the path that the birds eat. For others, and I hope for you, the seed will have germinated, so that you want to confirm that process, to set a marker in the earth by the young plant, to say: Here grows a Christian.

We all know what it means to confirm: it means to verify or corroborate or renew assent. Who is doing the confirming in a confirmation? Who is doing the verifying? There is no one straightforward answer to this, for it is really a three-way process. The individual confirms, the church confirms, and God confirms.

The individual says: Yes, I really do choose to call myself a Christian, I confirm the promises made on my behalf in baptism, I make my own public commitment to Christ. It is terribly important to say this, to stand up and be counted. Different Christian traditions have different ways of expressing this need – like the 'going up' of evangelical mass rallies – but confirmation is the traditional way. It is moreover a sacrament.

The second level of confirmation is by the church: the church confirms that it recognizes the individual as a full, committed member. That is why confirmation is normally done by a bishop, while baptism, which is more urgent, is done by a priest or in emergencies by a lay person. (The Catholic Church recognizes the validity of baptism by the laity, and a friend of mine in Kenya was baptized in an emergency by a layman who was a leper, which is doubly beautiful.)

Public recognition by the bishop adds a new dimension of seriousness to the commitment. Christians, after all, are not just pew-fodder; they are expected to do some work – to witness to the faith, explicitly, implicitly, in whatever way is appropriate to their possibilities. Everyone has some kind of an apostolate. The church needs you, its work depends on you.

The third level of confirmation is by God the Holy Spirit, as the paraclete, the strengthener, gives us grace to make us fit for the challenges of adult Christian life. In Catholic theology a sacrament is described as an outward sign of inward grace, that is, a symbolic action that reflects a new gift of God to us. We can see the bishop lay his hands on the confirmation candidates, and we can hear him speak of the gift of the Spirit. What we cannot see or hear is that gift of the Spirit, the imparting of grace. But the fact that the Spirit is invisible does not mean it is not a reality. The gift of the Spirit is like the roots in the earth – hidden from our sight, but the precondition for the green shoots that will soon be so visible and so beautiful.

The scripture texts chosen for confirmation habitually speak of the Spirit of wind and fire, but in many ways the sower is a more helpful biblical image. People don't usually feel the Spirit as a rushing wind or a flame on the head. They don't usually feel any dramatic change at all at their confirmation. I certainly didn't. We can be left with a disappointed sense that our confirmation is a one-off ignition that did not quite fire.

But there is a very good reason for this – confirmation is but a confirmation. It is not a complete new beginning, but a corroboration of what is already there. Seeds grow slowly. The parable of the sower helps us to see confirmation rather as a barely perceptible strengthening that grows firmer and firmer, year after year, as the roots thrust down further. Whoever can observe roots growing or blossoms opening, except in speeded-up films?

And so consider your confirmation, whether it is a past event or a future one, as a threefold opportunity. Firstly, as a chance for you to confirm your personal commitment to Christ. Secondly, as a moment for the church to confirm its recognition of you as a full, adult member. And thirdly, as a time for the Holy Spirit to confirm you with new strength. Can there be a better period of your life than your student years for such a threefold confirmation of who you are and of who you are going to be?

CHAPTER TWELVE
On My Bed at Night I Sought Him

Jeremiah 26.1–16; Psalm 4; Acts 3.1–10

> When you are disturbed, do not sin; ponder it on your beds, and be silent. (Psalm 4.4)

Today I have chosen to talk about the psalm, rather than about one of the prose readings.

We spend one third of our lives in bed, as the advertisements remind us. Hopefully, most of that time we are peacefully asleep, refreshing and renewing ourselves, and benefiting from what Macbeth called

> Sleep that knits up the ravelled sleave of care,
> The death of each day's life, sore labour's bath,
> Balm of hurt minds, great nature's second course,
> Chief nourisher in life's feast. (*Macbeth* 2.2.38ff.)

But it is not always like that, it is not always stillness and peace and sleep. Bed is also a place of wakefulness: a place of anxiety where worries assume monstrous dimensions, a place of anguish where tears wet our pillows, a place of nakedness where desire takes us over, a place of secrecy where we think and do those things that we want no one to know about except those who know and love and understand us best. A place where God has 'searched me and known me' – searched out 'my lying down' – the God to whom 'night is as bright as the day' (Psalm 139.1, 3, 12).

And so darkness becomes also a time of prayer. A couple of

weekends ago I stayed with Benedictine nuns at Stanbrook Abbey and was struck afresh by how much of the monastic office is sung in the darkness – either in the long hours before the dawn (vigils and lauds) or in the evening hours of darkness (vespers and compline).

Umberto Eco evokes the extraordinary power of these night offices in *The Name of the Rose*, when light struggles to dispel a little of the darkness, controlled singing breaks the silence of the night, and hope and trust in God does battle with the fears of the obscurity. Eco writes of how

> the office of matins takes place when night is still total and all nature is asleep, for the monk must rise in darkness and pray at length in darkness, waiting for day and illuminating the shadows with the flame of devotion.

This prayer in the night can lead to a

> sweetness no one can comprehend who has not experienced those hours of mystic ardor and intense inner peace. (*The Name of the Rose*, Picador, 1984, pp. 102, 103)

We know that prayer of darkness when we celebrate evensong in chapel in the winter evenings. The huge expanses of stained glass make the darkness a strong experience – not something we keep out with curtains, but something we have constantly alongside us as we pray.

Night and death are closely associated throughout Christian tradition. And so at evensong there is always the *Nunc Dimittis*, Simeon's song of peaceful acceptance of his death, after he has held the saviour in his own arms. 'Now lettest thou thy servant depart in peace, according to thy word, for mine eyes have seen thy salvation which thou hast prepared before the face of all people, to be a light to lighten the gentiles, and to be the glory of thy people Israel' (*Book of Common Prayer*, Luke 2.29–32).

Death and night are associated also in the two great suppers of Jesus: the night Supper at Bethany, when the Christ, which means 'the anointed one', received a memorable anointing for his burial (Mark 14.8), a powerful experience in which the house was filled with the smell of the costly perfume (John 12.3) and the woman's love overflowed into endless kisses (Luke

7.45). Shortly afterwards, the night meal in the upper room, the Last Supper, looked forward to Jesus' death: 'This is my blood of the covenant, which is poured out for many' (Mark 14.24).

And as the darkness thickened and the night progressed, Jesus tossed restlessly in his agony of Gethsemane, full of the fears of the night while others slept. Less than twenty-four hours after that, his body was laid in the tomb, hurriedly before darkness fell. This inspired the beautiful prayer of compline:

> O living God, in Jesus Christ you were laid in the tomb at this evening hour, and so sanctified the grave to be a bed of hope to your people. Give us courage and faith to die daily to our sin and pride, that even as this flesh and blood decays, our lives still may grow in you, that at our last day our dying may be done so well that we live in you for ever.
> (Jim Cotter's version, *Prayer at Night*, Cairns publications)

'A bed of hope'. That restless hope in the night is evoked from the beginning to the end of the Bible. Right from Genesis 1 we hear that 'darkness covered the face of the deep', and the 'Spirit of God hovered' there, or according to other translations 'a wind from God swept over the face of the waters'. God calls the darkness Night, and creativity hangs there, in the darkness and the wind and the emptiness, waiting to bring living things to birth.

Then, in the last book of the Bible, we enter heaven, in anticipatory vision, and find ourselves in a place where not only will there be no more death (Revelation 21.4) but there will be no more night (22.5).

But if such is the promise, the way to it is through the darkness that makes us aware of how much we need God: as Isaiah says, 'the people who walked in darkness have seen a great light' (Isaiah 9.2). And it is in the night that Nicodemus comes to Jesus for his great conversation, in which Jesus evokes that powerful wind of the Spirit that we met in the darkness of Genesis 1. 'The wind blows where it chooses, and you hear the sound of it, but you do not know where it comes from or where it goes. So it is with everyone who is born of the Spirit' (John 3.8).

If darkness leads us to prayer, making us aware in the stillness of the night of our need for God, then we can understand why the Psalms evoke, again and again, our thoughts at night in our beds, as a way of speaking of our longing for God. And so we read in tonight's psalm:

> When you are disturbed, do not sin;
> ponder it on your beds, and be silent ...
> I will both lie down and sleep in peace;
> for you alone, O Lord, make me lie down in safety.
> (Psalm 4.4, 8)

And in other psalms:

> I lie down and sleep;
> I wake again, for the Lord sustains me. (Psalm 3.5)

> I bless the Lord who gives me counsel;
> in the night also my heart instructs me. (Psalm 16.7)

Many other psalms present the human spirit desiring God at night, crying out with a restless longing.

> O my God, I cry by day, but you do not answer;
> and by night, but find no rest. (Psalm 22.2)

> My soul thirsts for God,
> for the living God.
> When shall I come and behold
> the face of God?
> My tears have been my food
> day and night. (Psalm 42.2–3)

> My soul waits for the Lord
> more than those who watch for the morning,
> more than those who watch for the morning.
> (Psalm 130.6)

At the same time there is a trembling fear because he sees us in our nakedness:

> O Lord, you search me and you know me,
> you know my resting and my rising ...
> O where can I go from your spirit,
> or where can I flee from your face? ...

If I say: 'Let the darkness hide me
and the light around me be night',
even darkness is not dark for you
and the night is as clear as the day ...
Already you knew my soul,
my body held no secret from you
when I was being fashioned in secret.
(Psalm 139.1, 7, 11–12, 14–15, Grail inclusive language
    version)

But even the language of the Psalms is surpassed by the passion
of longing in the Song of Solomon (Song of Songs):

Upon my bed at night
I sought him whom my soul loves;
I sought him, but found him not;
I called him, but he gave no answer ...
(Song of Solomon, 3.1)

I slept but my heart was awake.
Listen! My beloved is knocking.
'Open to me, my sister, my love ...'
My beloved thrust his hand into the opening,
and my inmost being yearned for him.
I arose to open to my beloved,
and my hands dripped with myrrh,
my fingers with liquid myrrh,
upon the handles of the bolt. (Song of Solomon, 5.2–5)

The collect of evensong asks God to 'defend us from all perils
and dangers of this night'. Yet the silent loneliness of the night
has a purpose: it can make us aware of our deep passions and
our human vulnerability. We should cherish what St John of
the Cross called the dark night of the soul, because through it
we discover desires we never knew we had. The thoughts that
pass through our heads as we lie on our beds can drive us
relentlessly to remember (in St Augustine's famous words at the
opening of his *Confessions*) that our hearts are restless until they
rest in God.

God comes to us by night, forgiving our sins, dispelling our
darkness, quietening our anxieties, soothing our anguish,

accepting our nakedness, fulfilling our desires. It is that confidence that enables us, this day and every day, to praise him. And it is that confidence that enables us tonight and every night, to lie down in peace and take our rest. For it is in God alone that we dwell unafraid.

CHAPTER THIRTEEN

Daniel and Zacchaeus – Figures for Today

Daniel 6.1–23; Luke 18.35 – 19.10

The story of Daniel in the lions' den is an old-time favourite. People think it suitable for children, because it has animals in it, and they teach it at Sunday school. It lies behind the well-known poem by Hilaire Belloc 'Jim, who ran away from his Nurse and was eaten by a Lion.' In case you cannot quite remember how that highly memorable poem goes, I'll recap the central section:

> He hadn't gone a yard when – Bang!
> With open jaws a lion sprang,
> And hungrily began to eat
> The boy: beginning at his feet.
> Now, just image how it feels
> When first your toes and then your heels,
> And then by gradual degrees,
> Your shins and ankles, calves and knees,
> Are slowly eaten, bit by bit.
> No wonder Jim detested it!
> No wonder that he shouted 'Hi!'
> The honest keeper heard his cry,
> Though very fat he almost ran
> To help the little gentleman.

But being eaten by a lion has not always been so funny. The early Christians were thrown to lions in much the same way as Daniel was – as a punishment for worshipping the God of

Jesus instead of the Emperor. In early Christian art, Daniel in the lions' den was a favourite theme. Not only did it give them courage to live through their experiences of persecution, but it was one of a number of Old Testament stories which acted as a pre-figuring of the salvation from death found in Christ.

Other Old Testament figures for eternal life expressed in catacomb painting and on early sarcophagi were Noah's salvation from the flood-waters of death, Jonah's salvation (after three days) from being swallowed by a whale, and the salvation of the three faithful Jews (Shadrach, Meshach and Abednego) from the fiery furnace, which is told earlier on in the book of Daniel.

In the ancient portrayals, Daniel is customarily shown standing with a lion seated symmetrically on either side of him, like rather beautiful bookends. There is a wall painting like this in the catacomb of SS Marcellinus and Peter, dated at the end of the third century, with DANIEL written in capital letters at the top. A naked figure holds out his hands in the customary attitude of prayer at the time, known from the Latin as the 'orante' position – this is still the posture that a priest uses at Mass when he prays aloud before the people. The lions sit on either side, stretching out their tails for balance; they are not looking at all sleepy, but very alert, with mouths open, but each is lifting up a paw of friendship.

A number of sarcophagi from the fourth or fifth centuries show similar scenes: a sarcophagus at Pisa has Daniel naked, with a lion on either side not touching him. On a sarcophagus at Ravenna, there is a very similar scene, but this time Daniel is clothed, though he still lifts his arms in the orante position.

Sometimes an additional detail is shown, and it comes from chapter 14 of Daniel, which is a Greek addition found in the Apocrypha. An angel appears to the prophet Habbakuk and tells him to take bread to Daniel in the lions' den, who – in this version of the story – stays in the lions' den for six days. Habbakuk calls 'Daniel! Daniel! Take the food that God has sent you,' and Daniel replies, 'You have remembered me O God and have not forsaken those who love you.' On sarcophagi at Arles, at Brescia and at the Catacomb of Callixtus at Rome,

Habbakuk is shown bringing sacred bread to Daniel as he stands between the two lions. It is a prefiguring of the eucharistic food that the early Christian artists portrayed as the bread of immortality.

A stone capital in a twelfth-century church at Souillac, in the Dordogne, echoes the traditional theme. The two lions have very manifest claws, but Daniel has his arms outstretched in what would earlier have been called the orante position, but this time his two thumbs are set right into the mouths of the lions and his fingers curl around their jaws, emphasizing how totally safe he was from their attack.

Death in a lions' den or being burned alive was no distant reality for the early Christians. One writer on catacomb art pointed out:

> In the picture of Daniel or the three Hebrew children the early Christians saw a divine pattern of the trials which lay on their way to the final triumph, the union with Christ. In a sense, the Bible with some of its most dramatic stories stepped right into their lives. (*The Catacombs*, edited and enlarged by Alfred Heidenreich from *Die Katakomben* by Emil Bock and Robert Goebel, Christian Community Press London, 2nd edition 1962, p. 34)

For us, today, lions have different associations. They are, after all, amongst our favourite animals. We speak of a pride of lions, the king of beasts, the courage of a lion's heart, the rich beauty of a lion's golden mane, and the glorious dominance of the lion's share. For us, the story of Daniel in the lions' den will arouse different feelings.

Within the tide of contemporary theological thinking, the story of Daniel in the lions' den belongs most naturally to that strand known as creation theology, that is, theology that stresses ecological concerns. Christianity, despite its Franciscan tradition, has not always had a good reputation for environmental awareness, and sometimes the blame is laid, rather unfairly, at the door of the Bible, because of the teaching in Genesis 1.28, when human beings are given 'dominion over the fish of the sea, and over the birds of the air, and over the cattle, and over all the wild animals of the air'. If this is misinterpreted, people can think that because they are the summit of creation they can do what they like with the rest of the world. Because they have dominion over creation, they can think the world is given to them to use exactly as they wish.

Recent theological work has repudiated this reckless attitude as a distortion of what is intended rather as the responsibility of trustworthy stewards. Theologians today draw attention to those biblical passages, and they are numerous, which promote the idea of environmental harmony. Take, for example, the ringing promise of the harmonious coexistence of creation in Isaiah 11:

> The wolf shall live with the lamb,
> the leopard shall lie down with the kid,
> the calf and the lion and the fatling together,
> and a little child shall lead them.
> The cow and the bear shall graze,
> their young shall lie down together;
> and the lion shall eat straw like the ox.
> The nursing child shall play over the hole of the asp,
> and the weaned child shall put its hand on the adder's
>   den.
> They will not hurt or destroy
> on all my holy mountain;
> for the earth will be full of the knowledge of the Lord,
> as the waters cover the sea. (Isaiah 11.6–9)

Daniel in the lions' den belongs to this tradition, a tradition in which people do not hurt animals and animals do not hurt people, for all live with respect for the rest of God's creation, a creation which God has seen to be good. Because Daniel worships God, his sense of humble reverence is sensed by the lions, who greet him as a friend to be lived with, not an enemy to be feared. As the Cambridge theologian Janet Martin Soskice has expressed it, the Old Testament stories of Adam and Eve and Cain and Abel show how 'violence spreads from the human realm to that of the animals. In the garden the animals live peaceably with Adam and Eve and with each other. After the Flood, we are told, they dread them. The point of these stories is that sin keeps us not only from right relation to other people but from right relation to the whole created order' (*Readings in Modern Theology*, edited Robin Gill, SPCK, p. 65).

Daniel tells the story of salvation from a manifest physical danger, but the reading from Luke's gospel which we heard tonight tells the story of salvation from sin. Whereas Daniel has no doubt that he needs salvation as he is plunged into the lions' den, Zacchaeus is in a very different situation. He is well off. There is nothing obviously wrong with his life, other than that he might like to be a little taller. He may be closer to the situation facing most of us. If someone says to us, 'Would you like to be saved?' then most of us, most of the time, do not cry out in desperation 'Oh thank God for that', but rather feel like replying with a certain frostiness, 'I don't need to be saved, thank you.'

Zacchaeus was much like that; someone who thought he was doing very nicely, thank you, until he met a man who changed his vision of the world. His life is turned around in the course of a day, to the point where he declares, 'half of my possessions I will give to the poor'. He went far beyond the demands of the Jewish law. Leviticus 6.5 and Numbers 5.7 said that money taken by defraud should be repaid plus one fifth of the capital; Zacchaeus says he will 'pay back four times as much'. He is a man in love with the new values he has encountered in Jesus, values that overwhelm him with the sheer goodness of their appeal.

The story of Zacchaeus is a story that reminds us that Luke's gospel is good news to the poor, fairly and squarely about the redistribution of wealth. It is a message of blistering relevance to a country that occupies itself with talk of tax cuts and of wealth cascading through the generations.

'Half of my possessions I will give to the poor'. Luke talks not of the spiritually poor, but the materially poor. Jesus announces his mission in Luke 4 as to bring 'good news to the poor' (v. 18). In Luke 6 his version of the Beatitudes begins 'Blessed are you who are poor, for yours is the kingdom of God' (v. 20). In Luke 7 Jesus gives as evidence that he has been sent by God the fact that 'the poor have good news brought to them' (v. 22). In Luke 14 Jesus says 'when you give a banquet, invite the poor' (v. 13). In Luke 16 Jesus tells the parable of the poor man lying at the gate of a rich man: the poor man went to heaven and the rich man to hell (v. 19–31). In Luke 18 Jesus tells the rich young man to 'sell all that you own and distribute the money to the poor' (v. 22). And then in Luke 19 Zacchaeus is inspired to give half his possessions to the poor. This is salvation not just for the poor, who will get the money, but for Zacchaeus himself, who will become a nicer person: 'Today', says Jesus, 'salvation has come to this house'.

We may or may not like the message, but it cannot be glossed over in talk of spiritual poverty. The gospel's option for the poor is the message that led the indigenous Peruvian theologian, Gustavo Gutiérrez, to say in his epoch-making book first published in 1971, *A Theology of Liberation* (English translation published by Orbis, 1973), 'Luke is the evangelist who is most sensitive to social realities' (p. 297).

He continues,

> It is impossible to avoid the concrete and 'material' meaning which the term *poor* has for this evangelist. It refers first of all to those who live in a social situation characterized by a lack of the goods of this world and even by misery and indigence. Even further, it refers to a marginalised social group, with connotations of oppression and lack of liberty. (p. 298)

And so, the old biblical stories take on a new face of meaning in every generation. The fear of persecution and martyrdom which once gave a cutting edge to the story of Daniel, now gives way to a burgeoning awareness of the unified harmony we are called to re-establish between humanity and the created order, through the insights of creation theology. And in a society of rapidly escalating inequalities between rich and poor, it is liberation theology that can draw our attention to the contemporary relevance of the story of Zacchaeus.

May God grant that our ears may not be closed, neither to the word of God in the Old and New Testaments, nor to the theologians of our modern day who are struggling to make the Good News better known.

CHAPTER FOURTEEN

Warfare in the Bible

1 Kings 22.1–17; Romans 15.4–13

When I looked up today's reading, I have to admit I was shocked. In 1 Kings we have the unappetizing story of King Ahab, hesitating over whether to make war on the Arameans.

He consults four hundred prophets to see if God will bless his enterprise with success. One of the prophets puts horns of iron on his head and says 'with these you shall gore the Arameans till they are destroyed'. All the other prophets say the same: 'Go up and triumph; the Lord will give it into the hand of the king.' Only one is out of step, the prophet Micaiah. At first he says the same as the others, and then he changes his tune. And suddenly, in the last verse of the reading, we are surprised to hear: 'I saw all Israel scattered on the mountains, like sheep that have no shepherd.'

We are surprised not so much because Micaiah has contradicted the other prophets, as because the verse is so familiar. Yet we know it from a totally different context – not the setting of war and bloodshed, but the merciful care of Jesus in Matthew's gospel. 'When he saw the crowds, he had compassion for them, because they were harassed and helpless, like sheep without a shepherd' (Matthew 9.36). We come across the familiar, comforting image of the flock and the shepherd at every Anglican evensong, when we say of ourselves: 'We have erred and strayed from thy ways like lost sheep.'

The theme of Jesus as good shepherd is one that is open to sentimentality – a blond-haired, blue-eyed, white-robed shepherd cradling a cuddly little lamb. There are so many such pictures of Jesus that this kind of pastoral idyll image must be familiar to us all. Yet here in 1 Kings the text about scattered sheep lacking a shepherd throws up quite different associations – associations of warfare, of bloodshed, of fear.

While tonight's reading stops at the scattered sheep verse, the story actually continues in quite an unpleasant vein. In fact the scholar commenting on this passage in Peake's classic *Commentary on the Bible* (Nelson, 1962, commentary by J. Mauchline) accuses it of 'immature theology and an unethical conception of prophecy': how is that for a text to preach on! The prophet Micaiah explains the contradiction between his message and that of the other prophets by saying that God intended to deceive Ahab so that he would be killed in battle, and therefore the Lord put a lying spirit into the mouth of all the other prophets.

For his pains, King Ahab has Micaiah imprisoned and fed with bread and water. Then he goes out into battle, and is struck by an arrow that slides between his scale armour and his breastplate. 'The battle grew hot that day, and the king was propped up in his chariot facing the Arameans, until at evening he died; the blood from the wound had flowed into the bottom of the chariot.' The people brought the body back and then: 'they washed the chariot by the pool of Samaria; the dogs licked up his blood, and the prostitutes washed themselves in it' (1 Kings 22.35, 38).

If we look up other Old Testament texts that are evoked by Matthew's 'sheep without a shepherd' verse, we again run up against blood and gore. In Ezekiel, God reproaches the prophets of Israel for being bad shepherds, with the result that the sheep 'were scattered, because there was no shepherd; and scattered, they became food for all the wild animals' (Ezekiel 34.5). Being a lost sheep does not just mean sitting on a mountain ledge until you are carried home on the shoulders of your rescuer: it means being torn apart and eaten. The shepherd, far from drifting around in a white robe, is a war hero, the one who defends you against enemies, protecting your life as you walk through the evil valley of the shadow of death (Psalm 23.4).

Then there is the book of Numbers, when Moses appeals to God to appoint someone to lead the Israelites in his place, since he is not to be permitted to enter the promised land. Someone is needed ' "who shall go out before them and come in before them, who shall lead them out and bring them in, so that the congregation of the Lord may not be like sheep without a shepherd." So the Lord said to Moses, "Take Joshua" ' (Numbers 27.17–18).

So far so good. But if you then open the book of Joshua and read what he did, you will find yourself in one of the most difficult, bloodthirsty parts of the Bible. I once made the mistake of choosing this little known book as my meditation material during a long holiday: I had to abandon it, as I read how Joshua struck town after town with the edge of the sword and left no one remaining (cf. Chapter 10).

Why does the Bible contain such bloody, warring passages? Perhaps there are two reasons: firstly, war is such a prevalent reality that scriptures which ignored it could not speak to the depths of the people's need. God is still God, whether we live in peace or are slaughtered in war. A Bible without war passages would indeed present us with a sentimental pastoral idyll. Secondly, war confronts us in a very acute way with issues of death and life, of meaning and meaninglessness, of fear and hope, of grief and thankfulness. Perhaps these reasons explain why so much of the greatest literature of the world is concerned with war.

A few years ago I saw Peter Brook's extraordinary adaptation of the Indian epic, the *Mahabharata*, performed on television. It was epic in its length as well as its style, and went on through the middle of the night. But far from falling asleep or feeling alienated I found myself gripped. Most dramatic of all was the conscience-searching that afflicted the characters on the eve of the great battle – an exploration into the ultimate meaning of life that was only possible amidst the heightened perceptions of staring death in the face, and on a massive scale.

Then there is Homer's great epic, the *Iliad*, which many people regard as greater than his peacetime epic the *Odyssey*. Its greatness does not come about through idealizing war: on the contrary, the memorable bits are the expressions of inconsolable grief, like the passage where Andromache mourns over the body of her husband Hector:

White-armed Andromache, holding the head of Hector killer of men between her hands, gave them the first lament:

'Husband, you were too young to die and leave me widowed in our home. Your son, the boy that we unhappy parents brought into the world, is but a little baby .... And you, my child, will go with me to labour somewhere at a menial task under a heartless master's eye; or some Achaean will seize you by the arm and hurl you from the walls to a cruel death, venting his wrath on you because Hector killed a brother of his own, maybe, or else his father or a son. Yes, when he met Hector's hands, many an Achaean bit the dust of this wide world.' (*Iliad* XXIV.723–37, translated E. V. Rieu, Penguin Classics, 1966)

Or there is the first player's speech in *Hamlet*, which tells of Hecuba 'the mobled queen', in the same war, running up and down dressed only in a blanket.

When she saw Pyrrhus make malicious sport
In mincing with his sword her husband's limbs,
The instant burst of clamour that she made –
Unless things mortal move them not at all –
Would have made milch the burning eyes of heaven
And passion in the gods. (*Hamlet* II.2.543–9)

The first player is so moved as he says these lines that he weeps and cannot continue.

In our day, when war is a matter of dropping bombs from high up, we do not always see the full horror of those sights of which these great writers spoke, nor share in the full alertness of perception that such dangers can lead to, when there is mutual risk of life in reciprocal combat. Yet we *sometimes* see the horror. This passage by Robert Fisk, writing during the Gulf War about the slaughter on the road out of Kuwait City, is not so different from 1 Kings in its account of the dogs licking the blood of King Ahab, or from Ezekiel in its account of the sheep being torn apart by wild animals. Fisk wrote:

It is a road of horror, destruction and shame .... At one

point on the highway yesterday, I saw wild dogs tearing to pieces the remains of Iraqi soldiers . . . . Corpses lay across the highway beside tanks and army trucks. One Iraqi had collapsed over the carriageway, curled up like a foetus, his arms beside his face, a neat moustache beneath a heavy head, the back of which had been blown away.

Only when ambulance drivers arrived and moved his body did we realise that his left leg had also gone. In a lorry which had received a direct hit from the air, two carbonised soldiers still sat in the cab, their skulls staring forward up the road towards the country they never reached. (*The Independent*, 2 March 1991)

In such writings about war, perhaps we miss the point if we ask, 'But whose side was God on?' just as we miss the point of the *Iliad* if we ask, 'But whose side was Homer on?' It is simply the wrong question. After all, our reading from 1 Kings tonight is largely devoted to explaining just how difficult it is in times of war to discern what God's will is – hence the conflict among the prophets, and Micaiah's confused and contradictory utterances.

Perhaps the point is rather this: that in war we know supreme vulnerability, supreme anguish, supreme fear, and, in such vulnerability, anguish and fear we have a supreme awareness of our need for God.

A prayer that comes at the end of Anglican evensong is for 'peace in our time . . . because there is none other that fightest for us, but only thou O God'. That image, of the only one that fights for us, is what the metaphor of the good shepherd should evoke in us – the one who pits himself against the threatening wolves, who casts out evil spirits to cure people of life-threatening illnesses, the real Jesus of Matthew's picture.

To say God is for us, should not be crudified into saying God is against the rest. God is, certainly, against our enemies. But only God knows who or what are our true enemies.

That evensong prayer for peace in our time, is followed by a collect for peace that goes still more deeply into the ways in which we can find God in the longings aroused in us by war or by the fear of war:

Give unto thy servants that peace which the world cannot give: that both our hearts may be set to obey thy commandments, and also that by thee we being defended from the fear of our enemies may pass our time in rest and quietness; through the merits of Jesus Christ our Saviour. Amen.

CHAPTER FIFTEEN

Love your Enemies

Jeremiah 29.1–14; Psalm 23, Philippians 3.7–21

When we hear scripture read in church there is a natural tendency towards a feeling of *déjà vu*. It all sounds so much like what scripture always sounds like, both in language and ideas, that sometimes it is hard to pay any fresh attention to the reading at all. So we often switch off and wait for the next item on the programme.

We might have had that sensation as the passage from Jeremiah 29 was read. Here is another prophet rabbiting on again, on the usual lines. In that case, it will come as something of a surprise to hear the opinion of one commentator, that the 'letter to the exiles' of Jeremiah 29 'contains so much that is novel and unprecedented ... that the prophet must himself have been surprised by the words that he wrote' (John Paterson, *Peake's Commentary on the Bible*, Nelson, 1962) .

How so? Jeremiah himself refers to a tension with the views of other Jewish prophets: he says they are deceiving the people and proclaiming a lie. Religion is not a series of cosy truisms, it is fraught with fierce opposition of ideas. We can see that in our own day: take the battle between the pro-gay and the anti-gay lobby within the churches. What was the equivalent point of controversy in Jeremiah's day?

The point of issue then was how to find God and be true to the faith while the people were in exile. For the Jews, the city of Jerusalem was all important. This was where the temple was, the sacred place where God could be truly worshipped. Later, Jerusalem was to be the place to which Jesus travelled every year – at first with his parents and later with his travelling companions, including the women who followed him (see Luke 8.1–3) – to fulfil the religious duties that could only be carried out in that seat of God's presence. Jerusalem was the heart of the promised land. It was crucial to Jewish faith that God's will was for his chosen people to live in Israel and to worship him in Jerusalem.

A wonderful passage from the end of Isaiah expresses, through some rich maternal symbols, the Jewish idea of Zion (that is Jerusalem) as their mother, to the point where God becomes identified with the mother who is Jerusalem:

> Rejoice with Jerusalem, and be glad for her
> all you who love her ...
> that you may nurse and be satisfied
> from her consoling breast ...
> you shall nurse and be carried on her arm,
> and dandled on her knees.
> As a mother comforts her child,
> so I will comfort you;
> you shall be comforted in Jerusalem. (Isaiah 66.10–13)

But now, as Jeremiah wrote, a group was in exile in Babylon, taken prisoner by Nebuchadnezzar. The Jewish exiles felt not only the distress that any refugee feels, but anger and resentment at the thwarting of God's will for his people. And their hatred of Babylon led them to riot and defy their enemies.

Yet Jeremiah tells them to stop being awkward. He tells them to settle down, build houses, plant gardens, get married and build families, even in their exile from Jerusalem. More than that he tells them to pray for the welfare of their enemies and of their enemies' city: 'pray to the Lord on its behalf, for in its welfare you will find your welfare' (v. 7). This injunction to pray for their enemies was a hard saying in the context of Jewish tradition, and it is without parallel in the Old Testament.

In this text we see the birth of a new idea, which will be developed later on by Jesus in his famous saying of Luke 6: 'Love your enemies, do good to those who curse you, pray for those who abuse you .... If you love those who love you, what

credit is that to you? For even sinners love those who love them'
(vv. 27–8, 32).

I have never forgotten hearing an elderly man from Eastern
Europe explain why he became a Christian: because Jesus said
'love your enemies'. He admired many other religious thinkers
and writers and philosophers but there was no one else who had
said anything more challenging, more difficult and more
profoundly right. When I find myself in a situation where I
need to argue the case of Christianity I always feel this is our
most persuasive card: that Jesus was the one who said 'love your
enemies'. And he lived out himself his own injunction when he
said of those crucifying him, 'Father, forgive them, for they
know not what they are doing.'

It was a particularly hard saying within the context of the
Old Testament, but it is a hard saying for us too. It goes against
all our instinctive inclinations. And yet it is profoundly healing.
We may not know how to love our enemies or even quite what
it means. Never mind, the first step is concrete enough: to pray
for our enemies. Even before looking at them, smiling at them,
or offering them a hand, we can hold them up in our hearts
before God and ask God to help them. It can lead to more, but
in itself it is enough for us to know we are at one with God.

In praying for enemies, praying for those who have hurt and
damaged us, possibly irrevocably, bitterness begins to melt and
true comfort begins. 'As a mother comforts her child, so I will
comfort you.' Religion is often said to give us comfort, and it
does, but it is not the deceptive comfort of lulling us into a false
sense of security. It is the tough, creative comfort of healing and
reconciliation.

The Holy Spirit is sometimes called the Comforter – as in the
well-known hymn 'O Comforter draw near'. This is the
Comforter whose comfort lies not in giving us everything we
feel like, but in kindling love in our hearts.

> Come down O love divine . . .
> Within my heart appear,
> And kindle it, thy holy flame bestowing.

Another of today's readings is the most famous psalm of all,

Psalm 23. It has become such a favourite because it is so associated with comfort.

> The Lord is my shepherd, I shall not want . . .
> Even though I walk through the darkest valley,
> I fear no evil;
> for you are with me;
> your rod and your staff –
> they comfort me. (Psalm 23.1, 4)

There are enemies in this psalm: they do not get their way, but they are not harmed, rather they are disarmed by the witness of God's love for his people:

> You prepare a table before me
> in the presence of my enemies;
> you anoint my head with oil;
> my cup overflows. (Psalm 23.5)

If God is for us, who can be against us? Jeremiah advocates a positive and cooperative attitude, but he does not abandon the traditional faith. Is it God's will that the people should be in exile from their homeland? This is another form of the classic problem of pain, and the answer is, 'No, of course not!' Jeremiah continues:

> Thus says the Lord: only when Babylon's seventy years are completed will I visit you, and I will fulfil to you my promise and bring you back to this place. For surely I know the plans I have for you, says the Lord, plans for your welfare and not for harm, to give you a future with hope . . . . I will let you find me, says the Lord, and I will restore your fortunes and gather you from all the nations and all the places where I have driven you, says the Lord, and I will bring you back to the place from which I sent you into exile. (Jeremiah 29.10–11, 14)

This is no pie-in-the-sky, passive fatalism. There is a will of God for us, and it is not for our hurt or diminishment, it is for our earthly good, it is for the Jewish return to Jerusalem.

The point is that while waiting for that will of God to be fulfilled in due course – seventy years, according to Jeremiah –

we can still find God in the diminished circumstances of our life. We can learn and grow through adversity, though God does not will us adversity. The great message that the Jews were invited to learn through their periods of displacement – both wandering in Egypt and the exile in Babylon – was compassion for the refugee. In the words of Deuteronomy: 'You shall love the stranger, for you were strangers in the land of Egypt' (Deuteronomy 10.19).

May those of us who have not had to endure the pain of exile, learn that lesson without having to become refugees ourselves, without being compelled to know at first hand what it feels like.

'I was a stranger and you welcomed me,' said Jesus (Matthew 25.35). When we have acted in such a way that those words can be said to us, then we can be welcomed into the homeland that is even more sacred, and more comforting, than Jerusalem. Then we shall, in the words of Psalm 23, 'dwell in the house of the Lord for ever'. Then we shall, in the words of Paul to the Philippians (from the second reading), find 'our citizenship in heaven'. Then we shall, in the words of the hymn 'O Comforter draw near', become the place 'Wherein the Holy Spirit makes his dwelling'.

LENT

CHAPTER SIXTEEN

Ash Wednesday

Joel 2.12–17; Psalm 51; Matthew 6.1–6, 16–18

Today we remember that we are dust, and unto dust we shall return (Genesis 3.19). It is the first day of Lent, a period traditionally of dust and ashes, sackcloth and mourning, fasting and penance – all rather unfashionable practices.

Not quite as unfashionable as they used to be, however, in the sixties and seventies. I believe a new asceticism is afoot. Take Friday abstinence, the practice of not eating meat: twenty or thirty years ago this was a weird practice that served only one purpose – to mark out Catholics as peculiar and different, a badge of the clan. Yet today look how many people have given up meat, restricting themselves to fish and a vegetarian diet. And they feel their little abnegation is a healthier and more moral way of life.

Or take sleep. Look how everyone is told how much better it is for them to sleep on a hard mattress. The newer your bed the more uncomfortable it is. It is quite impossible to buy those soft beds of the past into which you sank as though into feather-down.

Or take silence. When I was at school a silence detention was the most savage sort of punishment that could be imposed. The whole school would file into the assembly hall and stand there in total silence for twenty minutes before being allowed home. Now silent retreats have become popular. With televisions, radios and stereos in every room, people can think of the prospect of a communal silence as a blessed relief from the constant hammering of noise.

Or take fasting. Think how much money people will spend

on going to a health farm and being ritually starved of most things except carrot juice and bran flakes for a week. It is something so difficult that they could not do it on their own. And yet they come away again feeling so good, so pure, so improved, so whole, so healed.

In ways like this we are beginning to understand again what Lent is about, and to catch the first glimpse of why today is an echo of the ritual of the book of Joel, in which fasting is something solemn and purposeful and holy:

> Blow the trumpet in Zion;
> sanctify a fast;
> call a solemn assembly;
> gather the people.
> Sanctify the congregation . . . . (Joel 2.15–16)

Ash Wednesday is the day we think about our mortality. Psalm 103 puts this beautifully:

> As for mortals, their days are like grass;
> they flourish like a flower of the field;
> for the wind passes over it, and it is gone,
> and its place knows it no more.
> But the steadfast love of the Lord is from everlasting to
>   everlasting . . . . (Psalm 103.15–17)

Another moving expression of mortality is found in the short but poetic book of Ecclesiastes:

> Remember your creator in the days of your youth, before the days of trouble come, and the years draw near when you will say, 'I have no pleasure in them'; before . . . the silver cord is snapped, and the golden bowl is broken, and the pitcher is broken at the fountain, and the wheel broken at the cistern, and the dust returns to the earth as it was, and the breath returns to God who gave it. (Ecclesiastes 12.1, 6–7)

These are poignant verses. But meditation on our death is not only a practice for Christians, quite the contrary. The Buddhists practice a meditation on the corpse, which may initially shock you, but which brings a surprising and liberating sense of peace. At least, that has been the experience of everyone I have known to practice it. The Buddhists call it a reality meditation. In the version presented by Anthony de Mello in *Sadhana* (Gujarat Sahitya Prakash, 1978), you imagine your own corpse at nine different stages.

1. First the corpse is cold and rigid.
2. Now it is turning blue.
3. Now cracks appear.
4. Decomposition sets in in some parts.
5. The whole body is in full decomposition.
6. The skeleton now appears with some flesh adhering to it in some places.
7. Now you have only the skeleton with no flesh on it at all.
8. Now all that exists is a heap of bones.
9. Finally, the bones are all reduced to a handful of dust.

What is confusing, I think, is whether one is supposed to be happy or miserable about all this dust and ashes and fasting. Jesus tells us not to play up the misery. 'Whenever you fast, do not look dismal, like the hypocrites ... they have received their reward. But when you fast, put oil on your head and wash your face' (Matthew 6.16–17).

Just as the meditation on the corpse brings peace rather than depression, even in the depths of its hard facing of reality, so too we find a similar ambivalence in a diary entry by an eighteen-year-old girl, Jane O'Shaughnessy, in the last weeks before her death from leukaemia:

> I am told that I am dying ... I am not angry or bitter. I am in surprisingly good spirits. I joke, I laugh. It has not affected me in the sense that I'm depressed. I've even been told off for not being depressed ... I do have my days of sadness – but not depressant sadness – a sort of pleasant peculiar sadness more filled with a warm sort of love and tenderness, like a soft rain.

Love is the key to understanding. It is when we love that we find ourselves joyfully accepting abnegation. Perhaps losing our appetite if we are in love. Perhaps denying ourselves beers or chocolates to save up our money for travelling to see the person we love. Perhaps getting up in the night to feed a baby we love.

Fasting and mourning, sackcloth and ashes, they are all meant to stimulate love. They are inspired by love, and they are meant to lead to greater love. To break open our hearts.

That is where our motivation lies. We cannot naturally enjoy fasting, or giving up alcohol or chocolate, or reflecting on our mortality, or giving alms to the poor, or rising in the night, or spending time talking to beggars, or depriving ourselves of conversation or music, or receiving ashes on our foreheads. They are hard and we can only find the strength for them in a greater love.

How on earth did Jesus find the strength to go into the desert to fast for forty days – that period of which our Lent is a pale reflection? Only because he was burned up by passionate love of God and the desire to do nothing else but to dwell in it.

How can we find the strength to love others? It is easy if we are in love, or if we have children, or even if we have friends, but it is hard to deny ourselves for the sake of those we do not know. Only a passionate love of God can give us the motivation we need to see others as our sisters and brothers. Inside every one of us a God-shaped hole, a yearning that grows fiercer the more we notice it is there. As St Augustine said: 'You made us for yourself, and our hearts are restless until they rest in you' (*Confessions*, 1.1).

It is this love which inspired the most beautiful prayer by St Ignatius, from his Contemplation for Attaining Love:

> Take Lord and receive all my liberty, my memory, my understanding, and my entire will, all that I have and possess. You gave it all to me; to you Lord I give it all back. All is yours, dispose of it entirely according to your will. Give me the grace to love you, for that is enough for me. (*Spiritual Exercises*, 234, in *Saint Ignatius of Loyola: Personal Writings*, trans. Joseph A. Munitiz and Philip Endean, Penguin Classics, 1996)

Becoming aware of that hunger for God can overshadow our other hungers just a little, so that the priorities of our lives change, even as we accept our penances. That single-hearted search, with sacrifice, is called purity. And that reward of wholeness and health and cleansing is called peace. And that desire for God we are nourishing this Lent – as we deny ourselves our other desires – is called love. So, as we bear just for one evening upon our bodies the ashes of repentance – the outward reminder of our mortality, the withered flower of our lives to which the everlasting steadfastness of God stands in such contrast, the dust from which we have come and to which our bodies shall return – we are nourishing love. And it is all we need.

CHAPTER SEVENTEEN

Repent

Deuteronomy 6.1–9; Hebrews 4

> Hear therefore, O Israel, and observe them diligently, so that it may go well with you, and so that you may multiply greatly in a land flowing with milk and honey. (Deuteronomy 6.3)

Yesterday I took part in a Historical Decade Dinner of the Catholic Women's Network, where we drank milk and shared honey-cake. As we passed the cup of milk we said, 'Go forth and be sustained', and as we passed the honey cake we said, 'Honeycake for the promised land'. And we remembered our foremothers, those who had gone before us through the wilderness, on the journey to the promised land: people from history and myth, from the present and the ancient world. Women such as St Verena, who cleaned lice out of the hair of the poor; Christine de Pisan, the only woman writer of the fourteenth century to make a living from her pen; Eglantine Webb, who founded Save the Children and inspired the children's rights' legislation that we have; Etty Hillesum, the Dutch Jew whose diaries show such faith in God as she moved towards the concentration camp where she died; and Maya Angelou, the strong and inspiring black poet of today.

In Lent, which we have now entered, we live again the wilderness period, the trial and temptation period, the austerity and penance period, and we look towards the promised land of Easter for which we will have to wait some six weeks more. Because we are now in Lent I am going to do something rather unfashionable. I am going to invite you to repent of your sins.

That is a phrase that may sound quaint, awkward, embarrassing. But it is at the heart of our faith. When John the Baptist came, he prepared the way of the Lord by preaching repentance. When Jesus arrived in person, his first message of preaching (according to Matthew and Mark) was, 'Repent, for the kingdom of heaven has come near'. In John the first act of his active ministry was to cleanse the temple, throwing out sin even from what appeared most righteous.

Our society has become almost incapable of living a season such as Lent. I live opposite a Muslim family, who rigorously observe Ramadan, when neither food nor drink pass their lips during daylight hours. How strange that seems to our world. For us, Christmas begins in the shops in October and, once the Christmas goodies are finished, early January sees the coming of hot cross buns – which are a nice treat instead of a fasting food marked with a cross to remind of the passion of Good Friday. No sooner are we into Lent – the season of fasting – than chocolate eggs are all over the shelves. It is all feasting without fasting. All celebration without austerity.

Yet of one thing I am convinced. There is no faster, more direct route to intimacy with God than through being sorry for our sins. There is in repentance considerable pain and discomfort, but also intense joy and liberation as we allow ourselves to be stripped bare of all our habitual responses of self-justification. When we repent we allow ourselves, against our natural instincts, to say: 'I too am to blame, I caused hurt, I did not want to see, I acted for my own advantage, I was insensitive, I avoided responsibility, I put off the day of reckoning, I did wrong, I was negligent, I am sorry'.

Recall the words from the epistle to the Hebrews.

> The word of God is living and active, sharper than any two-edged sword, piercing until it divides soul from spirit, joints from marrow; it is able to judge the thoughts and intentions of the heart. And before him no creature is hidden, but all are naked and laid bare to the eyes of the one to whom we must render an account. (Hebrews 4.12–13)

God's gaze is at the same time loving and penetrating. Think of the arrow of love which pierces the heart of St Teresa of Avila.

Sister Wendy Mary Beckett, now famous as an art critic, wrote years ago about bringing ourselves before God in prayer:

> It is a terrible thing to be a fallen creature, and for most of the time we busily push this truth out of our awareness. But prayer places us helpless before God, and we taste the full bitterness of what we are. 'Our God is a consuming fire', and my filth crackles as he seizes hold of me; he 'is all light' and my darkness shrivels under his blaze. It is this naked blaze of God that makes our prayer so terrible. For most of the time, we can persuade ourselves that we are good enough, good as the next man, perhaps even better, who knows? Then we come to prayer – real prayer, unprotected prayer – and there is nothing left in us, no ground on which to stand. ("Simple Prayer", *The Clergy Review*, February 1978)

The famous psalm of repentance, known from its first word in Latin as the *Miserere*, begins:

> Have mercy on me, O God,
> according to your steadfast love;
> according to your abundant mercy
> blot out my transgressions.
> Wash me thoroughly from my iniquity,
> and cleanse me from my sin. (Psalm 51.1–2)

It continues, with a powerful juxtaposition:

> Let the bones that you have crushed rejoice. (Psalm 51.8)

Gerard Manley Hopkins, the great Jesuit poet, echoes that image in the opening lines of the 'Wreck of the *Deutschland*'.

> Thou mastering me
> God! giver of breath and bread;
> World's strand, sway of the sea;
> Lord of living and dead;
> Thou hast bound bones and veins in me, fastened me flesh,
> And after it almost unmade, what with dread,
> Thy doing: and dost thou touch me afresh?
> Over again I feel thy finger and find thee.

We are frightened of our nakedness before God. And we are frightened in the end not because God is cruel or vindictive – it is not so: God is tender and merciful, as trustworthy as the most understanding mother. What frightens us is ourselves, seen in the light of God's truth. So we run away. We push aside the seasons of self-examination, austerity and penitence, and buy early Easter eggs, forgetting what they are for.

But we cannot run away for ever. In the act of contrition used when I was a child I was taught to say that I was sorry for my sins 'because they deserve thy dreadful punishments, because they have crucified my loving Saviour Jesus Christ, and most of all because they have offended against thine infinite goodness'. That did not mean a lot to me then, and yet those three reasons, so old-fashioned in their expression, do encompass our three motivations for regret over what we have done: suffering punishment, seeing hurt to others, realizing the gap between others' goodness and our own lack of it.

We are driven to regret when the penalties of our actions fall upon us – when our drinking and driving leads to the loss of our licence; when our failure to budget lands us with a debt that weighs upon us; when our laziness leads to failing an exam that we needed to pass; when our petty theft lands us in jail. Punishment is tough and we can react with more stubborn embitterment, but sometimes it can shock us into a change of heart.

We are driven to regret also when our failures are seen to have hurt not just ourselves but others we love – when we find out just how much we have hurt our parents, our boyfriend or girlfriend, our children. Guilt is a part, an unavoidable part, of our response to the death of those close to us: that softness and generosity we held back from others in their lifetime, how willingly we would give it to them now it is too late.

We are driven to a humble realization of our shortcomings when we see someone who has qualities far surpassing our own, such that we cannot help but admire them, cannot help but admit our inadequacies in comparison. It is this, I think, that led to the standing ovations for Desmond Tutu when he came to Oxford. He was applauded not just for his speeches, but for what his presence stood for – perseverance and vision through circumstances that we knew would break or embitter us.

When we bring ourselves before God we have the same feeling, much more acutely. However much we have been in the habit of justifying ourselves beforehand, once we are faced with the purity of God we are filled with embarrassment at ourselves. It is this shame that leads Anglicans to make the famous prayer before the eucharist:

> We do not presume to come to this thy table, O merciful Lord, trusting in our own righteousness, but in thy manifold and great mercies.

Now that we are in Lent, I would like to make to you a suggestion, which of course you are perfectly at liberty to ignore. Decide on a time this week to set aside half an hour to review your life before God. Perhaps tonight, before you go to bed, you would like to lock your door and open your heart to God's gaze. Perhaps you have an essay crisis and another night would be better.

When you have found a time, ask for God's enlightenment. Tell God that you want to know what your sins are. That is a hard prayer to make, but once it is made you are halfway there. You want to know what your sins are, you want to be sorry, you want to be a better person, a kinder, braver, stronger, nicer person.

Then examine your conscience in the presence of God. You will only dare to face your sinfulness if you can trust the forgiveness of God. So remember the words of Hebrews this evening:

> We do not have a high priest who is unable to sympathize with our weaknesses, but we have one who in every respect has been tested as we are. (Hebrews 4.15)

There are several ways of doing an examination of conscience, but nothing is likely to come up unless you are willing to let God show you.

One good way is to look over the past: the past day, or week, or year, or the whole of your lifetime. Looking back, what have you done that you now are really happy about? It may well be

something that was a bit of a struggle at the time: a commitment to work that yielded results, time spent with people in
need. The other part of the exercise is the converse. What have
you done that you now feel uncomfortable about?

Another way of examining your conscience is to go down a
checklist. It can be a very basic guide, like the Ten Commandments, which you will find in Exodus 20.2–17, or the Beatitudes
from the sermon on the mount, which you will find in Matthew
5.3–12. It could be questions asked at the Last Judgement as
told in Matthew 25.31–46: have I fed the hungry? ... given
drink to the thirsty? ... welcomed the stranger? ... clothed the
naked? ... taken care of the sick? ... visited those in prison? If
not, how could I do these things, now or in the future? It could
be the checklist used by members of the Iona community,
which involves so many young Christians in Scotland: How
have I used my time, my treasures, my talents?

It is a good idea to write down what comes up, even if you
burn it afterwards. It makes the exercise more serious, and
becomes a form of confession.

Confessing is a very painful but cathartic exercise. Anglicans,
as well as Catholics, may make confession of their sins to a
priest. A friend of mine who had been away from the church for
several years said she was so drunk with joy after she had been
to confession that she did not know how she drove home. Or
you may prefer to confess to another Christian friend. In the
Middle Ages, when a soldier wanted to make a confession and
there was no priest available, he would sometimes confess to his
horse, or to his sword. It may sound comical, but it is a good
idea, because saying it out loud, like writing it down, helps to
make the process of contrition more real.

You will find that confessing not only helps express a sorrow
for sin, it also helps bring about a sorrow for sin. The point of
this exercise is not to be left in a permanent unease, but to
complete the stage of contrition through a definite act of
expression, so we can move ahead to the next stage: that of
living in gratitude because we accept that we have been
forgiven.

The old manuals used to speak of contrition, confession and
satisfaction. Satisfaction means making amends. Repentance

without change is a game. The only real satisfaction is made for us by Christ, but we unite ourselves to that sufficient act of satisfaction through doing our own little bit, restoring stolen property for example or making at least a token act of reform.

Lenten resolutions can be an excellent way of leading us along that long road of reformed habits, in which we become fractionally better people. Again, resolutions are best written down. And regularly, through Lent, or beyond, we should check up on ourselves. There are always things that we should do, that we know we should do, that we always mean to do, and that we will go on postponing for ever unless we pin ourselves down to a precise resolution.

Some resolutions, like giving up some item of food or drink for Lent, make satisfaction in a more generalized way. Small as these gestures are, they are highly valuable, for they help to awaken in us an awareness that our selfishness needs to be controlled.

Remember, repentance is the fast track to God. If we can open our heart, lay bare our soul, humbly submit ourselves to God's gaze, then we will find both pain and joy in those incisive words from Hebrews. Let us listen to them again:

> The word of God is living and active, sharper than any two-edged sword, piercing until it divides soul from spirit, joints from marrow; it is able to judge the thoughts and intentions of the heart. And before him no creature is hidden, but all are naked and laid bare to the eyes of the one to whom we must render an account. (Hebrews 4.12–13)

CHAPTER EIGHTEEN

Repenting of Anti-Semitism

Genesis 17.1–7, 15–16; Psalm 119.161–76; Romans 11.13–24

Today's two readings invite us to remember our Jewish heritage with pride. We gentile Christians are, in Paul's words, wild olive shoots grafted into the rich root of the cultivated olive tree, which is Judaism, taking the place of some of the original branches. We are reminded: 'Do not boast ... If you do boast, remember that it is not you that support the root, but the root that supports you' (Romans 11.18).

And yet the fact is that Christians have boasted of their position *vis-à-vis* the Jews. They have more than boasted. They have turned on the blood descendants of Abraham with despising and hatred. They have blamed them, as a race, for the death of Jesus, even though the Creeds have always taken care to say, 'He suffered under Pontius Pilate', and not, 'He suffered under the Jews'.

In this era after the Holocaust, when we have seen the horrific consequences of anti-Semitic attitudes, the Catholic Church conveniently tends to forget the facts about the origin of anti-Semitism.

To give just some facts: successive Popes expelled Jews from Rome in 1320, ordered the burning of the Talmud in 1322, burned alive a Franciscan friar who embraced Judaism in 1553, and, from 1555 onwards, set up an overcrowded Jewish ghetto in Rome, ordered the wearing of a Jewish badge (a yellow hat for men and a yellow kerchief for women), forbade the owning of property, compelled Jews to attend conversionist sermons, forbade the singing of psalms on the way to the graveyard, and forced Jews to take part in a race down the Corso to the jeers of the crowd. The injustice of the ghettos only came to an end in the capture of Rome by the forces of united Italy in 1870.

It is sinister to recall the similarity of this to Hitler's treatment of Jews, with the ghettos and the stars sown on jackets. That led ultimately to genocide, when between five and six million Jews were murdered in the concentration camps.

Many Catholics alive today can remember the church's official prayers every Good Friday for 'the perfidious Jews', removed from the liturgy only thirty years ago. The attitude was bred out of a racial resentment against the Jews, because they did not recognize Jesus as Messiah.

It was an approach that was the direct opposite of what Paul tells us in this passage of Romans. He, like Jesus, was a Jew, and he loved those who he called his 'flesh' (translated as 'my own people' in the NRSV, verse 14).

In preparation for the Millennium, Pope John Paul II invited Christians, and especially Catholics, to repent of the church's past sins. As one step towards that end he called a gathering of sixty experts, with some Protestant and Orthodox guests but sadly no Jews, to meet in Rome at the end of October 1997. The purpose was to study the church's complicity with the root causes of anti-Semitism, or rather what they called anti-Judaism (which focuses on hatred of the Jewish religion rather than of the Jewish race).

The meeting concluded that such attitudes had always been a distortion and a misunderstanding of the Christian position, though they had been derived from some erroneous interpretations of the New Testament. One such passage which had been misinterpreted was the cry of the crowd in Matthew's gospel: 'His blood be on us and on our children!' (Matthew 27.25).

Another source of distortion was the habit of the fourth evangelist to use the term 'the Jews' (for John, almost a technical term) to describe Jesus' opponents throughout the gospel. Some scholars have explained this term as meaning 'the Jewish leaders' or 'the Judaeans'. Undoubtedly John would have been horrified if he had known that his words would be taken as justification not just for a small and persecuted group of Christians to hold their heads high against the opposition of the religious authorities of the day but for a cruel reversal of the roles, in which the Christians become the dominant force and persecute all who are blood descendants of Abraham, extending this persecution into other historical contexts and other European nations.

The president of the Vatican commission, Georges Cottier, acknowledged that these 'pseudo-theological judgements which have circulated among Christian peoples for a long time' had 'served as a pretext for unjustifiable harassments'. They had 'suffocated the capacity for evangelical reaction', he said, 'when Nazi anti-Semitism, of a pagan and anti-Christian nature, swept Europe'.

Perhaps it was not enough of an apology; but it was something. Perhaps the children from every Christian school should study the history of anti-Semitic attitudes, and recoil with shame from the role the churches have played. But the meeting was a step in the right direction. A great deal of progress has been made in Jewish–Christian relations, and we should continue to build on it. In this season of Lent, it is appropriate that we should remember with shame and sorrow our part in this centuries-old anti-Semitism.

But repentance does not remain at the level of gloomy depression. The Greek word for repentance, *metanoia*, means a change of heart and mind. And so we can begin to rejoice in our new attitudes, and in the reconciliation between peoples that is brought by abandoning our old attitudes.

We can begin to be proud of that rich root of cultivation on to which we have been grafted. We can be proud of the Jewish race, because Jews are our adopted fathers and mothers, and we have been graced with their rich religious heritage. The religion of Jesus becomes our religion too – though sensitivity is needed in expressing this in an interfaith context, so that it does not appear that Christians are trying to take over Judaism or target Jews for conversion. But within our Christian self-understanding, we are all adopted Jews, and should be proud of it.

This brings us back to the first reading, from Genesis 17. The childless Abraham and Sarah are promised not just a son, but a multitude of nations as their descendants. We, by adoption, belong to that multitude of nations; Abraham is our father and Sarah is our mother.

We are not just biological children of Abraham, but heirs of Sarah too. We inherit a covenant of love, a chosen marriage commitment, for Sarah and Abraham were bound together in body and spirit, in a common Jewish faith and a mutual love and a shared hope in the promises of God. They were the first in a series of great matriarchs and patriarchs: Rebecca and Isaac, Rachel and Jacob.

I am reminded of the poignant moment at the end of the film *Schindler's List*, when the descendants of the Jews saved by Schindler come forward one after another, and each lays a small stone on his tomb. Some among them are survivors of the original group saved by Schindler – in wheelchairs, or on sticks – but together with them is a greater and increasing number of younger people and of children – the descendants. Without the original group saved by Schindler, none of these would be alive today.

Without Sarah and Abraham, none of us would be here in this chapel tonight. Without the Jewish people, and the wonderful faith they have bequeathed to us, none of us would be a Christian now. Our hearts may thrill as we feel included in the triumphant promises to that couple. We are part of God's gift to them.

To Abraham God promises, 'I have made you the father of a multitude of nations. I will make you exceedingly fruitful.' For Sarah, God's promise is 'I shall bless her, and she shall be a mother of nations; kings of people shall come from her.' And to both, and to their descendants, and to us, God promises, 'I will establish my covenant between me and you and your descendants after you throughout their generations for an everlasting covenant, to be God to you and to your descendants after you.'

Freed from the enmities of the past, we rejoice to be included in that everlasting promise, that God will be *our* God and that we will be God's beloved children and heirs.

For too long Christians have taken on an arrogant attitude towards the faith of the Old Testament, forgetting it is an integral part of our Bible, and making crude comparisons

between the primitive old attitudes of the Jews and the new
teachings of Jesus. But Jesus was not a Christian: he was a Jew.
He was the King of the Jews. He rejected nothing of his faith. In
bringing it to completion he did not write off a jot or a tittle
(Matthew 5.18), but helped illumine its inner meaning more
fully.

So it is appropriate that Christian monastic groups still make
the heart of their daily prayer the Psalter, as Jesus did. It is
appropriate that, as proud, adopted children of Sarah and
Abraham, we sing psalms at matins and evensong, uniting
ourselves spiritually with the persecution of the Jews, and with
the repentance of Christians. Listen to these words from the
psalm for tonight's evensong:

> Princes persecute me without cause,
> but my heart stands in awe of your words . . .
> I long for your salvation, O Lord,
> and your law is my delight.
> Let me live that I may praise you,
> and let your ordinances help me.
> I have gone astray like a lost sheep; seek out your servant,
> for I do not forget your commandments. (Psalm 119.161,
>   174–6)

CHAPTER NINETEEN

The Wrath of God

2 Kings 6.8–23; Luke 19.41 – 20.8

'If you, even you, had only recognized on this day the things that make for peace!' says Jesus, in tears, as he gazes down over Jerusalem. Jesus weeps because of the thought of the war to come: enemies setting up ramparts around the city, surrounding it, crushing the people and leaving not one stone upon another. This sack of Jerusalem happened in AD 70, and it is generally thought that the gospels reached their final form after this date.

It is, of course, a subject of fierce dispute what *are* the things we need to recognize which make for peace. It is not my business to subject you to my opinions on the subject of whether the British government should build closer relations with Sinn Fein, stop sanctions against Iraq, or negotiate with Argentina on the future of the Malvinas.

I am sure that there is great wisdom and holy example in Elisha's approach of giving food and drink to enemies instead of slaying them by the sword. But I am equally sure that the Old Testament reading tonight cannot be taken as proof that God is a pacifist.

It is worth pointing out that Jesus was no softie on the subject of peace. Jesus did not say 'Blessed are the peace-lovers', but 'Blessed are the peacemakers'. No sooner has he shed tears at the thought of the violence that will break over Jerusalem, than he enters the city, goes into the temple, and wreaks his own form of violence there. This is no gentle Jesus meek and mild, but a passionate young man. Luke, in fact, is very restrained in his reporting. In Matthew and Mark we are told that he overthrew the tables of the money-changers, and the seats of those who sold doves. In John we are told that he threw the money on the floor, and set to with a whip made of cords.

Imagine someone marching into the college chapel when it is full of people and behaving like that. This was more than a non-violent demonstration. It was a forcible eviction, executed with heat and anger and violence. It is hardly surprising the authorities came to him and demanded, 'by what authority are you doing these things?'

There are very few events in Jesus' life recorded in all four gospels – only his baptism, the feeding of the five thousand, the anointing at Bethany, the passion and resurrection, and also this incident, which is usually politely called the 'cleansing of the temple'. Its appearance in all four gospels means it was a highly important incident, historically beyond dispute, theologically of key significance.

Of course it is easy to concentrate on the theological and symbolic aspects, and that is a valid exercise. Theologically we can see the new saviour showing the time of old ritual prescriptions is coming to an end, with a breakthrough in relations between God and humanity. Similarly, a little later on, at the death of Jesus on the cross, the veil of the temple will be torn violently from top to bottom. But there is a danger in ducking the historicity of the cleansing of the temple to focus too exclusively on its theological symbolism. Then we spiritualize the event, and run away from the sheer violence and anger of the historical Jesus.

The violence of the scene is graphically presented in the film *Jesus of Montreal*. The young man playing Jesus loses his temper when a girlfriend is asked to strip for an audition. He throws the cameras to the ground and thousands of pounds worth of electronic equipment smash on the floor. The flashes and crashes of the electronic carnage bring home to us that Jesus is a sign of contradiction, a troublemaker whom people want to remove and will go to any lengths to remove.

What does this do to our picture of Jesus the peacemaker? Any answer to that must be an extremely personal one, but I have to confess my personal response is one of delight that Jesus behaved in such a way. Apart from anything else, it makes him so much more interesting. It adds depth and complexity to a figure whose gentleness is usually emphasized more than his controversial, revolutionary qualities. It rescues him from being soppy.

The compassion of Jesus the peacemaker is of course still there. He is still the healer who, in the poignant words of the hymn 'My song is love unknown,' 'made the lame to run' and 'gave the blind their sight'. The killing of Jesus was a monstrous injustice, because he was an 'innocent' man, as the centurion recognized at his death (Luke 23.47), 'a prophet mighty in deed and word' who was condemned to death, as the couple affirmed on the way to Emmaus (Luke 24.19).

But also true is that Jesus was a figure of such challenge that he could not be ignored. He had to be followed and worshipped, or cut down and crucified. In one sense, he would not go quietly, because his appeal was irresistible and his claims outrageous if they were not true. In another sense, he did go totally quietly, rendering absurd the show of arms brought to his arrest, walking to his death like a lamb to the slaughter, opening not his mouth.

Jesus was no cardboard cut-out of predictability. He often took his closest friends by surprise by his reactions of impatience or irritation. The same man who could tell Peter to forgive not seven times but seventy times seven (Matthew 18.22) could also turn on him in a sudden burst of anger and cry 'Get behind me Satan!' (Matthew 16.23). The same man who could raise Jairus' daughter from death (Mark 5.41) could also seem at first to reject the Syro-phoenician woman's plea for her child, telling her that it was not right to cast the children's bread to the dogs (Mark 7.27). The same man who absolved Mary of Bethany from cleaning up the kitchen and commended her for sitting at his feet as a male student would do (Luke 10.39) could also hurt her to the core of her being when he failed to come to Lazarus in his fatal illness. 'If you had been here', she reproached him, as she wept at his feet, 'my brother would not have died' (John 11.32). The same man who inspired his followers with confidence that he was the promised king who would save Israel, could also leave them baffled and scattered as they found him crowned with thorns and dead upon a cross.

The same child who was obedient to his parents in Nazareth, could also run away from them and remain lost for three days, leaving them wracked with worry (Luke 2.48–51).

On that occasion he was in the temple, which he called 'my Father's house'. 'Did you not know', he said, 'that I must be in my Father's house?' In the cleansing of the temple, he again uses the same phrase: 'Stop making my Father's house a market-place' (John 2.16).

We can excuse Jesus' strange action, by explaining that as the only-begotten Son of God he had special and unique responsibility for protecting the house of his Father. And such an explanation would be perfectly valid. But again, the danger is of explaining away Jesus, predicting him, packaging him, instead of allowing us to live in creative tension with a character whom we admire and revere but do not wholly understand. The deepest love comes out of the mystery of those unfathomed depths of his personality.

Again and again we are told in the gospels that the disciples of Jesus did not understand him: when he told the parable of the sower (Mark 4.13), when he performed the miracle of the loaves (Mark 6.52), when he said 'Where I am going you cannot come' (John 8.21, 22), when he said 'The truth will make you free' (John 8.32–3), when he entered Jerusalem on the colt of a donkey (John 12.15–16), when he prophesied his passion and resurrection (Luke 18.34), when he met the despondent couple on the road to Emmaus (Luke 24.45). On all these occasions, the disciples did not understand him. It is too trite to say that we now understand everything.

The attraction of Jesus is the appeal of a man with magnetic goodness and yet with soul-disturbing questioning. He leaves us baffled. He troubles our complacency. When he throws the tables and the money to the ground, he does not just overthrow the way of life of the Jewish moneylenders, he overthrows our way of life, in ways that we do not fully understand. And yet our instinct tells us that *he* is right and *we* are wrong.

It is worth saying one word more about anger. The wrath of God is a very unfashionable concept. But we are wrong to ignore it. When we assert the wrath of God we are asserting justice, not an anything-goes, shake-hands-and-be-friends, peace-before-justice kind of mercy. God does not make peace by backing down; God forges peace by forcing justice. There are things in this world so wrong, so wicked, so shameful, that there can be no reconciliation before there is the brokenness of repentance. And that may require fearful anger.

God is angry when the innocent are killed, whether through individual cases of cold-blooded murder or through the mass killings of international economic injustice in which we all bear some complicity. When we say God is angry, we remind ourselves that there is an urgent need to put things right. And when we say God is angry, in a strange sort of way we spread peace in our hearts. For if God is not angry, then frustration and tension is built up inside us, at the problem of evil, at the unfairness of things. If God is not angry, then someone else jolly well ought to be. We can even be driven to turn to God in anger, and cry 'Why do you allow it? Why aren't you angry? Don't you care?'

When we speak of the anger of God we assert our faith that if God has not yet intervened in the suffering of the innocent it is for no lack of sensitivity to right and wrong. If justice has not yet been done, then it damn well will be, in God's eternity.

One of my favourite psalms is the *Miserere*, which many people know best from its musical setting by Allegri. Some of the words of that psalm of repentance – words that I have quoted to you before now, because I find them so powerful – go like this:

> Against you, you only, have I sinned
>   and done what is evil in your sight . . .
> Purge me with hyssop, and I shall be clean;
>   wash me, and I shall be whiter than snow.
> Let me hear joy and gladness;
>   let the bones that you have crushed rejoice.
> (Psalm 51.4, 7–8)

There is both joy and crushing, both peace and violence, in the complexity and mystery and depth of our relationship with God.

May this Lent, this period of penance and reassessment, be for us a time for having our tables overthrown, our money scattered on the floor, our comfortable seats knocked over, our self-satisfactions driven from us by a whip of cords. And then, with bones crushed, with a broken spirit, with a broken and contrite heart, may we know the sheer joy of God's mercy.

CHAPTER TWENTY

The Pelican and the Lamb of God

Exodus 12.1–11; John 1.29–39

If we look around us at the walls and windows in any church or chapel, we find them full of rich symbols and fine art. The pictures and glass are there to lead us to a better understanding of our faith and a more rounded response to God, bringing into play not only our ears and our intellects but also our eyes and our imagination. It is perverse to ignore these visual images, when we spend so much time looking at them. So I have chosen to reflect today on the theological message of some of the works in Exeter College chapel in Oxford.

The most famous work is the tapestry of the Adoration of the Magi, made by William Morris to a design by Edward Burne-Jones. This original design showed a bare and hilly landscape behind the figures, contrasting with the patch of vegetation on which the mother and child are welcoming their wise visitors from afar. Morris kept the spirit of Burne-Jones's idea, but as he converted the sketch into a tapestry he substituted for the bare hills a dark forest background. In the night darkness, the flowers that surround the holy family are lit up by the light of an angel. There is a fairy-tale spirit to the tapestry, which captures the romance of our faith.

Another point that appeals to me in this William Morris tapestry is the way he has shown the magi. At least one, if not two of them, look so feminine they could be women. The word *magi* just means wise people, and though the word has a male ending, that need not indicate more than one man among the group. Often artists have shown at least one of the three as unbearded and rather effeminate. There is one painting in the Uffizi Gallery in Florence, by Lorenzo Monaco, which shows the third wise person as such a delicate figure, with even the suggestion of breasts, that it is very hard to look at her and not see her as a woman.

But the images I want to concentrate on today are the Salviati mosaics to either side of the altar. They were not original to the design by George Gilbert Scott, the architect of the chapel, but were installed in 1868, just nine years after the chapel was opened. In particular, as we approach Passiontide, I want to reflect on two mosaics which point to the sacrifice of Christ: the Lamb, on the left of the altar, and the Pelican, on the right.

The Lamb is an animal rich in theological meaning through-out the Bible. We can go right back to the ram stuck in a bush which Abraham killed as a sacrifice to spare the life of his son Isaac, in an early prefiguring of the sacrifice of Christ (Genesis 22.13).

But the key appearance of the Lamb in the Old Testament is in the story of the flight from Egypt. Moses told the Jews to daub their doorposts with the blood of a lamb, so that the angel of death would know to pass over their houses. Homes which were not marked with the sacrificial blood would lose their firstborn that night (Exodus 12.1–13). Lamb then became the regular food of the Passover meal, a constant reminder of the salvation history of the chosen people, who are redeemed from slavery into freedom, passing from death to life.

In the book of Isaiah the Lamb appears again, as an image of the docility of the Suffering Servant:

> He was oppressed, and he was afflicted,
> yet he did not open his mouth;
> like a lamb that is led to the slaughter,
> and like a sheep that before its shearers is silent,
> so he did not open his mouth. (Isaiah 53.7)

The Suffering Servant plays a sacrificial role, which brings salvation to the people:

He was wounded for our transgressions,
crushed for our iniquities;
upon him was the punishment that made us whole,
and by his bruises we are healed . . .
He bore the sin of many,
and made intercession for the transgressors.
(Isaiah 53.5, 12)

And so the Lamb, dumb before its slaughterers, is a figure for Christ. The first person to make this identification explicitly is John the Baptist, who points to Jesus right at the beginning of the fourth gospel, and says, 'Here is the lamb of God who takes away the sin of the world!' (John 1.29). The figure of John the Baptist, clad in his animal skins and pointing to Jesus, is a common one in iconography. Sometimes we even see John the Baptist as a chubby baby pointing to Jesus as another chubby baby (they were, after all, cousins), and the message is the same: 'Behold the Lamb of God'.

In the last book of the Bible, Revelation (which is written by the author of the fourth gospel or at any rate by his theological circle), the Lamb imagery resurfaces powerfully. This time we have the imagery of a heavenly scene, where twenty-four elders carrying incense and harps fall down before the Lamb and sing him a new song:

You were slaughtered and by your blood you ransomed
  for God
saints from every tribe and language and people and
  nation . . .
Worthy is the Lamb that was slaughtered
to receive power and wealth and wisdom and might
and honour and glory and blessing! (Revelation 5.9, 12)

A couple of chapters further on, a multitude appears robed in white and carrying palm branches. 'These are they', we are told, 'who have come out of the great ordeal; they have washed their robes and made them white in the blood of the Lamb' (Revelation 7.14). Washing robes white in blood is a strong and paradoxical image, throwing purity and violence into powerful juxtaposition with each other.

Every time we see a picture of a Lamb in church, these multiple, overlapping biblical references are evoked. Over centuries, from the earliest traditions to the last book of the New Testament, the Lamb has been a key figure for our salvation, resurfacing again and again to represent in different ways the innocent victim whose blood brings life to the world. The Lamb whom we see now, carrying his flag of victory, is Jesus Christ, killed in our place, risen victorious for our salvation, and now enthroned in heaven; and he brings along with him all the sacrificial prophecies and foreshadowings that cluster around the figure of the Lamb in the Old Testament.

But what about the Pelican? The Pelican is much less known as a figure for the sacrificial love of Christ. Yet once you begin to notice Pelican imagery, you will begin to notice it again and again, carved in stone, or painted on manuscripts, or in mosaic form as it is here. Understanding the symbolism of the image is essential to appreciating the artist's intentions.

Unlike the Lamb, the Pelican is not really a biblical image. Though it does make a skimpy appearance as an example of a wild creature found in desolate places in Psalm 102 (also echoed in Isaiah 34.11 and Zephaniah 2.14), the meaning of the Hebrew word is uncertain. While the Revised Version (still one of the most reliable, literal translations) has 'pelican', the Revised Standard Version has 'vulture', the New Revised Standard Version has 'owl', the New International Version 'desert owl' and the Good News Bible 'wild bird'.

With all this uncertainty about what is in any case a fleeting reference, it is sounder to base the use of the symbol not in biblical texts, but in ancient tradition. Its use goes back all the way to a book known as the *Physiologus* around 200 AD, which presents the tale of the mother Pelican wounding her own breast in order to feed her chicks.

This is what our mosaic shows. The Pelican points her long beak to pierce her own breast, and the drops of blood fall into the open mouths of the young birds, who are dying of hunger. It is easy to see why this became used as an image for Christ. The Pelican gives life to her children by feeding them on her own blood, as Jesus does in the eucharist.

In a number of illuminated manuscripts around the twelfth

century, the Pelican appears as a regular iconographical theme, building her nest on the top of the cross. This juxtaposition with the passion strengthens the connection between the shedding of Christ's blood in death and the life-giving power of the eucharist.

The first theologian to make a detailed exposition of the Pelican as a figure for Christ was St Augustine, who picked up the ideas of the *Physiologus* and developed them in the context of Psalm 102, which he evidently *did* take to be about a pelican. The psalm is similar to the famous passion psalm which Jesus quoted on the cross: 'My God, my God, why have you forsaken me?' (Psalm 22), and it goes like this:

> Hear my prayer, O Lord,
> And let my cry come unto thee.
> Hide not thy face from me in the day of my distress . . . .
> By reason of the voice of my groaning
> My bones cleave to my flesh.
> I am like a pelican of the wilderness;
> I am become as an owl of the waste places.
> I watch, and am become
> Like a sparrow that is alone upon the housetop.
> Mine enemies reproach me all the day.
> (Psalm 102.1–2, 5–8, Revised Version)

Augustine develops the Pelican as an image for the maternal qualities of Christ. Not only is the Pelican of the legend a mother bird fighting to preserve life in the midst of desolation, but Jesus uses the image of a mother bird of himself, and uses it in the same way – as a mother fighting to preserve life in the midst of desolation: 'How often have I desired to gather your children together as a hen gathers her brood under her wings, and you were not willing! See, your house is left to you, desolate' (Matthew 23.37–8). The complementarity of maternal with paternal imagery for God is important, says Augustine, for the Lord has fatherly authority but motherly affection (*En. in ps.* 101, 8, CC 40, 1431–2).

The idea of Jesus as mother was famously developed later on by Julian of Norwich, who builds on a very similar idea – the way a mother gives her children to feed on herself – though she does so without invoking the Pelican. 'The mother can give her child to suck of her milk, but our precious mother Jesus can feed us with himself, and does, most courteously and most tenderly, with the blessed sacrament, which is the precious food of true life.'

But the Pelican is not ignored by theologians, and the great master Thomas Aquinas made what is perhaps the best-known literary reference to the Pelican in his hymn on the eucharist, *Adoro te devote* ('Godhead here in hiding'). In a verse which is sometimes omitted because people do not understand it, Aquinas addressed Jesus directly and bluntly as 'Holy Pelican, Lord Jesus':

> *Pie pellicane Jesu Domine,*
> *Me immundum munda tuo sanguine.*
> *Cuius una stilla salvum facere*
> *Totum mundum quit ab omni scelere.*

In Gerard Manley Hopkins' translation, this runs:

> Bring the tender tale true of the Pelican;
> Bathe me, Jesus Lord, in what thy bosom ran,
> Blood that but one drop of has the world to win
> All the world forgiveness of its world of sin.

So the Exeter chapel walls present us with two complementary creatures as icons of the sacrificial Christ, the Lamb and the Pelican. One stresses gentle innocence and silent vulnerability, the other loving self-sacrifice in a desolate world. One represents the Suffering Servant, the other the life-giving Mother. Both shed their blood that others may live.

Sacrifice is a much-maligned concept these days. People recoil from the suggestion that God demanded the death of his Son, and they reject the promotion of self-sacrifice as an ideal for womanly submissiveness. But that is to miss the point. Sacrifice is what we do for those we love, not because it is demanded or idealized, but simply because we love them.

Sacrifice is when a mother gets up in the night to feed her baby; or when a man goes out to work to save up for a plane ticket to see his girlfriend; or when a wedding couple choose to vow themselves to each other 'for better for worse, for richer for poorer, in sickness and in health, till death do us part'; or when grown-up children make a rota to stay up through the night with a parent who is dying. Sacrifice is when we give our life for others, which is what every girlfriend and boyfriend does, every wife and husband does, every mother and father does, every daughter and son does, in a myriad different ways.

Sacrifice is not wrenched from us kicking and screaming, but is a gift, freely offered, with the innocent gentleness of a lamb, or the loving warmth of a mother. Such is the gift of Jesus Christ to us, and it is life-giving.

CHAPTER TWENTY-ONE

The Anointing of Jesus

Isaiah 52.7–10; John 12.1–8

The story of the anointing of Jesus by a woman is one of the great mysteries of our salvation, and yet it has received scant attention from the church. We do not set aside a special day to celebrate the anointing in the way that we celebrate other key mysteries from Jesus' life: the Epiphany or the baptism of the Lord, the entry into the desert or Palm Sunday, Maundy Thursday or the Ascension.

Yet the anointing is at the very heart of our faith. The word Christ, after all, means 'the anointed one', so the moment at which Jesus receives his anointing is of crucial importance for revealing who he is. Sometimes theologians have described his baptism as the moment of his anointing in a metaphorical sense: as he is baptized with water he is anointed with the Spirit. But a far clearer, more evident, moment of his anointing is when he is physically anointed at the hands of a woman.

It is perhaps no surprise that what a woman did has been seen as unimportant. The American biblical scholar, Elisabeth Schüssler Fiorenza, comments scathingly on the way this story has been marginalized:

Although Jesus pronounces in Mark: 'And truly I say to you, wherever the gospel is preached in the whole world, what she has done will be told in memory of her' (14.9), the woman's prophetic sign-action did not become a part of the gospel knowledge of Christians. Even her name is lost to us. Wherever the gospel is proclaimed and the eucharist is celebrated another story is told: the story of the apostle who betrayed Jesus. The name of the betrayer is remembered, but the name of the faithful disciple is forgotten because she was a woman. (*In Memory of Her*, SCM, 1983, p. xiii)

Yet the anointing is one of the very few events recorded in all four gospels, which is another measure of its significance. The only other events to appear in all four gospels are the baptism of Jesus, the feeding of the five thousand, the entry into Jerusalem, the cleansing of the temple and the passion and resurrection cycles.

Strictly speaking, the anointing belongs to the passion cycle, and this is recognized at least by Bach, who begins his St Matthew Passion in the house of Simon the leper at Bethany, where Matthew sets the anointing. In Matthew, Mark and John the anointing is the immediate trigger to the sequence of passion events – provoking Judas to go to the chief priests with an offer of betrayal – and it takes place at Bethany (Matthew 26.6–13, Mark 14.3–9, John 12.1–8). In John, however, it is in the house of Martha and Mary, not that of Simon the leper. In Luke the anointing is placed earlier in the gospel; it takes place in the house of a Pharisee, but he is still called Simon (Luke 7.36–50).

In Matthew and Mark the woman is unidentified; in Luke she is identified as a sinner; and in John she is identified as Mary of Bethany. In Matthew and Mark Jesus is anointed on the head; in Luke and John he is anointed on the feet. In Matthew and Mark the meaning of the anointing centres around preparation for the passion; in Luke and John – though in very different ways – it is an expression of gratitude. All these accounts, different as they are, build up a rounded picture of a single mystery so rich in its significance that we seem never to exhaust its meaning.

Some of the most evident meanings of anointing, drawing from Old Testament tradition, and all of them deeply relevant to the approaching passion of Christ, are these. Anointing can be the sign of a prophet, for Elijah anointed Elisha to be a prophet (1 Kings 19.16). It can be the sign of a priest, for Moses anointed Aaron and his sons to be priests (Exodus 30.30). And it can be the sign of a king, for Samuel anointed Saul, and David after him, to be a king (1 Samuel 10.1, 16.13). How rich and solemn, then, is this holy moment when Jesus is consecrated to take on the fullness of his messianic role, to take forward his ministry as priest, prophet and king, even unto death on a cross. There, crowned with thorns as 'King of the Jews', he will make the priestly offering of his life, and point the direction to the new era of the Spirit.

Since Elisabeth Schüssler Fiorenza wrote her book, feminist scholars have tended to prefer the accounts from Matthew and Mark. But when I wrote my book on New Testament women, *Six New Gospels* (Geoffrey Chapman, 1994), I followed the fourth gospel account, to build up a fuller picture of Mary of Bethany (who is, of course, quite a different person from Mary Magdalene). John's version is also richest in its description of the smell of the ointment permeating through the whole house. Aromatherapy is now often used as a therapy for the ill and the dying, and it is beautiful to recall Mary of Bethany massaging this sweet-smelling oil into the feet of Jesus.

Luke's version has tended to fall out of favour among feminist scholars, because of the description of the woman as a sinner. Yet it can be a powerful account to read at moments when we need to hear Jesus saying to us, 'Your sins are forgiven'.

Luke and John, with their anointing of the feet of Jesus, may remind us of the lines of Isaiah made famous in Handel's *Messiah*: 'How beautiful are the feet of them that preach the gospel of peace'. The words are nowadays perhaps almost as well known in the form found in the hymn 'Our God reigns', which is in fact a substantially faithful translation of Isaiah 52.7–10.

> How lovely on the mountains are the feet of him,
> who brings good news, good news,
> announcing peace, proclaiming news of happiness:
> our God reigns, our God reigns!

> You watchers, lift your voices joyfully as one,
> shout for your King, your King,
> see eye to eye, the Lord restoring Zion,
> our God reigns, our God reigns!

Waste places of Jerusalem, break forth with joy,
we are redeemed, redeemed.
The Lord has saved and comforted his people:
our God reigns, our God reigns!

Ends of the earth, see the salvation of your God,
Jesus is Lord, is Lord.
Before the nations, he has bared his holy arm:
our God reigns, our God reigns!

That hymn says that Jesus 'brings good news', and the same phrase is found at the beginning of Jesus' ministry in Luke, when he stands up in the synagogue at Nazareth and applies to himself the prophecy from the beginning of Isaiah 61 (v. 1):

The Spirit of the Lord is upon me,
because he has anointed me to bring good news to the poor. (Luke 4.18)

The talk of bringing good news shows that the intimate scene of Luke's anointing also has a missionary dimension, if taken in conjunction with the passage from Isaiah. The woman anoints the feet of Jesus with fragrant ointment to make them beautiful, so that he will be the king walking on the mountains and bringing good news to the poor. Travelling is hard work, a blistering task for feet, but it is consecrated as a holy enterprise by the anointing of the feet.

Ahead of us as we approach Holy Week lies the monstrous offence against Jesus' feet when they are nailed to the cross. Even this sacrilegious moment is prepared for as his feet are now anointed with love. 'How beautiful are the feet'. The anointing is a preparation for the passion, blessing in advance the parts of the body that are to suffer so much.

It is also an anticipation of the moments after his death, when his body will be taken down in a hurry and shut in the tomb before the onset of the sabbath at sundown. The fragrant oils for dead bodies are applied now, in anticipation of the anointing that will never happen in the three days before dusk on Good Friday and first light on Easter morning. The women will bring spices to perform the anointing on Easter morning, but it will be already too late.

Yet the Jesus who will elude us at the tomb can yet be honoured on this earth. From Matthew and Mark's accounts we learn that when we no longer have Jesus to anoint in person we will always have the poor to anoint in his place. The Brazilian theologian, Dominique Barbé, put it like this:

> When my body is no longer with you, when I shall no longer be visibly there, the poor will take my place and it will be they whom you must perfume, that is, help in every way and overwhelm with the perfume of your love. (from *Grace and Power*, Orbis, 1987, p. 20)

As we share spiritually in the very physical act of the woman's grateful anointing today, we find ourselves doing more than simply saying 'Thank you'. We find ourselves entering mystically into the very salvific process. For we are consecrating Jesus for his preaching work, the mission to bring good news to the poor, and for his redemptive work, the gift of his life on Calvary. We unite our hands with the woman who anointed the anointed one, and who sent him off, loved and blessed, on the path to his passion and on the road to the world's salvation.

THE EASTER SEASON

CHAPTER TWENTY-TWO

It is the Lord

Numbers 13.1–2, 17–33; John 21.1–14

The gospel reading today is so famous and so beautiful that it is hard to say anything that will do it justice. John 21, otherwise known as John's epilogue – because certain textual features make it read like a later addition – is one of those favourite passages that Christians cherish.

Why? Firstly, because it is about the resurrection – the climax and the king-pin of our faith. There are not a great number of resurrection appearances, so each one is precious. Secondly, because – like all of John's texts – it is imbued with theological significance. Thirdly, because it is told with vivid and sensual detail. I shall deal with these three points in turn.

Easter is far from over. We are in the middle of it, still building up to the great triumph of the ascendancy of Christ on Ascension Day. The joy of the resurrection renews the whole world, and renewal of its nature must go on and on. The *triumph* of Easter comes with a mighty clash, with an angel from heaven and an earthquake and the rolling away of the stone. But the *joy* of Easter seeps in by degrees, as the fear and terror of Mark's women at the empty tomb gradually gives way to the barely trusting hope of Luke's disciples, who 'disbelieved for joy' (Luke 24.41).

That in turn gives way to the slowly-settling peace of John: Jesus has to repeat his words 'Peace be with you' (John 20.19, 21). And that in turn gives way to the quiet concentration of the days of prayer in the upper room. And then to the new explosion of enthusiasm that sent the disciples out to tell the world at Pentecost.

Within that process of growing joy we now stand. This is the happiest time of the year, and the beauty and warmth of the spring echoes the happiness of our hearts. Everything works together for good, everything will come right in the end, because Jesus Christ is risen. Even pain and death cannot stand between us and everlasting happiness. Because he lives, we too shall live.

The disciples move from puzzlement to joy when they actually see Jesus risen. The appearances make their resurrection faith not just a generalized celebration of the perpetual rebirth of all nature, but a personalized resting in the presence of one they love.

This appearance is in Galilee (the northern part of the country, where Jesus grew up), not in the Jerusalem region, where most of the other appearances are situated. John's account here concurs with the angels' promise in both Matthew and Mark: 'he is going ahead of you to Galilee; there you will see him' (Mark 16.7, cf. Matthew 28.10), and with the final appearance of Jesus on a mountain in Galilee at the end of Matthew. (In Luke, by contrast, there are no post-resurrection appearances in Galilee.)

The miraculous catch of fish in this story of John's is similar to the miraculous catch of fish after a whole night's unsuccessful fishing, early in Luke. That was when Jesus first called Peter and the sons of Zebedee: 'from now on you will be catching people' (Luke 5.10). Whether there were two such miracles, or whether one of them has been transposed in time, from ministry to post-resurrection or vice versa, the point seems to be this: Christ can be found by going back within your own life, back to the simple everyday things, back to the people you know, back to your roots. The romance of the faith is not only in mission and travel and danger in strange lands; there is also the freshness of discovering God in the land you came from.

We know that Peter and the others did become missionaries, did travel, did lose their lives far from home preaching to the gentiles. Yet for that very reason there is something precious about this story of how they found Jesus back home, back where they first met him, back in the work they were doing before they became apostles.

The story has other echoes too. The bread and fish eaten on the beach remind us of the bread and fish of the feeding of the five thousand, which is told in all four gospels. In the version of the story found in the fourth gospel, the miracle of the loaves is presented clearly as a eucharistic pointer, culminating in the strong and provocative teaching: 'I am the living bread that came down from heaven. Whoever eats of this bread will live for ever' (John 6.51). The fourth gospel is the only one not to include the institution of the eucharist at the Last Supper, but John's eucharistic faith is made quite clear in that 'eucharistic discourse'.

With these theological associations in mind – the finding of Christ back home, and the eucharistic resonances – we are set to recall the unfolding of the story. No one writes more movingly of the resurrection appearances than the fourth evangelist, with his Mary Magdalene in the garden turning at the sound of her name, and his doubting Thomas putting his hand intimately into the wounded side of Christ. And now we have this delicately painted chapter 21, evoking warm, grilled fish on a beach in the cool light of dawn.

One of St Ignatius's favourite prayer exercises, which he called the 'application of the senses', is to let the five senses become active in the imagination as we read a scene from the gospels. No story is better suited to that method than John 21. It opens with a snatch of dialogue. We hear Simon Peter saying, in that simple way he had said it hundreds of times before, 'I am going fishing.' We hear his friends reply, and we join them in saying, 'We will go with you', as though to say to the rock on which Christ founded his church, 'We will go along with you in preaching the gospel.'

We see the darkness of the long hours of night, and feel the tiredness of limbs that have been rowing and hauling nets without reward. We hear the silence of the night, bar the rhythmic slapping of wave against boat. We smell the saltiness of sea air and feel the hunger of a stomach after a night up without nourishment. We feel the disappointment of long waiting.

Dawn breaks. We have all the time in the world to watch the pinkness of the sky make its patterns, and to see the transformation of a world of greys into a world of colours. As visibility returns we see a figure far off on the beach. We hear the distant shout across the hundred yards that separate us: 'Children, have you any fish?' And we hear the authoritative words that we feel no desire to question or reject: 'Cast the net to the right side of the boat, and you will find some.'

We feel the weight of the nets now bursting with fish, so different from their feel before. We hear the cry of joyful recognition by the beloved disciple, 'It is the Lord!' We feel the splash of water as Peter jumps into the cold water.

On the beach now there is the warmth of a fire and the red and blue play of its flames. There is the sweet and welcome smell of fish grilling. There is the numbness of the brain after a night up, a brain that is happy to do the simple repetitive task of counting fish, one by one. There are 153 – one of John's characteristic details of irrelevant exactitude that make a scene come alive. And 'though there were so many, the net was not torn' – yet another small sign of resurrection promise as though to say that the coming church can take in huge numbers without damage.

And then those amazingly ordinary words, so precious by their apparent banality, so familiar, so welcoming: 'Come and have breakfast.' And finally the most sensuous moment of all, as in our imaginative memory we eat crumbly, freshly baked bread and crumbly, warm, charcoally fish. We pray with our mouths, but not in words, rather in the communion of eating. We are praying in that we are consciously enjoying the presence of Christ.

That presence of Christ can be ours, now in the resurrection era, over and over and over again. We are the Easter people, and Alleluia is our song. Happy Easter.

CHAPTER TWENTY-THREE

If You Love Me, Feed My Sheep

Ezekiel 34.1–16; John 10.1–18

A happy Easter to everyone. This season of the resurrection goes on and on, and Easter happiness increases weekly as the summer grows warmer, from the fear and amazement at the empty tomb, to a joy that knows no bounds and that cannot be contained, but drives us out to share the good news with all the world. I share in that joy with you.

Today's readings speak of the good shepherd, and it must be admitted that despite our Easter good mood, it may be that our first, instinctive reaction to good shepherd imagery is not one of unabated enthusiasm. The good shepherd is too often associated with twee Anglo-Saxon portrayals of a blue-eyed blond-haired youth with a lily-white lamb on his shoulders. For an urban society, the pastoral imagery can be mythical and sugary.

There is another reason too why some of our first associations with shepherd imagery may be negative ones. The role of the pastors, or shepherds, of the church has often been seen in an oppressively clericalist light. You do this or that, believe this or that, because your pastors tell you, and they claim to know because they have the role of guiding you along the right path and saving you from errors.

It is sometimes said that the sheep are supposed to look up and be fed, but instead they look down and are fed up. I remember hearing a sixth-former saying without a trace of irony that the church's teaching was that the laity ought to behave like sheep. We know how sheep behave, mindlessly following what all the rest of the flock do, as they are pushed by the shepherd or the shepherd dog to one side or another. A religion that tells people to behave like sheep is not likely to be viewed in high esteem by students at university.

The role of the bishop is based on that of a shepherd, and his crozier is shaped like a shepherd's crook for that reason. Yet the church's pastors are too often seen, not as those who lead the flock into lush pastures, but rather as those who keep them from lush pastures, firmly telling them that the unpalatable grass is better for their digestion.

Why have pastors got themselves a bad name in so many parts of the world? One of the reasons has been the explosion of cases of sexual scandal concerning clergy and even bishops that have come into the open in so many countries, England included, this diocese included. People have felt betrayed, hurt and disillusioned, as case after case of sexual abuse has come out into the open.

It is no longer credible to speak in simplistic terms of following the lead of the pastors. Invoking the model of the good shepherd no longer carries conviction as a reason why the shepherds' behaviour should be unquestioned. Trust has been lost. It cannot be regained by bullying. It cannot be regained by pastors appearing to protect other pastors more than they protect the flock.

There is a need to reaffirm what is right and what is wrong for a pastor to do, in terms other than 'what the pastors do is right, because it is the pastors who do it'. There is a need for pastors to admit that they belong to the sinful body, and do not stand outside it, even making a public confession – as some bishops, both Anglican and Catholic, have done in recent years. When a shepherd admits that he is not just a guiding pastor but also an erring sheep, he does not lose trust, he gains it.

Yet despite the blows that the image of the pastor has suffered, we cannot duck the idea of the good shepherd. In fact this is one image in the Bible that comes up again and again, from the historical books to the prophets of the Old Testament, from the gospels to the epistles of the New Testament. What we need to do is return to those biblical roots, rather than let our picture be dominated by the distorted image of pastoring that has built up over the centuries.

First of all, the image of the blue-eyed, blond-haired shepherd of the lily-white sheep is, biblically, a nonsense. In Palestinian Judaism, shepherds, with their roving life, were suspect figures, seen as thieves and cheats, the bottom rung of society. When the God of the Old Testament is hailed in the words, 'The Lord is my shepherd', there is all the tension of a challenging metaphor.

When the shepherds are the first to be told of the birth of the king in the middle of Christmas night, the message is one of good news to the poor, of the upside-down nature of this kingdom where the first to pay homage are the rascals of this world, where the light shines in the darkness and the night becomes bright as day. Who are those awake at night? Only those with an essay crisis, struggling to get it done in time; or those in labour to bring a child to birth; or the night-workers who serve us, keeping open our emergency services. The life of a real shepherd is no country idyll; it is hard, rough, austere and sometimes brutal.

The two passages we heard tonight from Ezekiel and John are crucial ones, revolutionary ones, for understanding what is meant by true pastoring of the flock. Ezekiel opens with a scathing denunciation of the failures of the official pastors. Instead of feeding the flock, they have fed off the flock. They have not strengthened the weak or healed the sick or gathered the scattered, but 'with force and harshness you have ruled them' (Ezekiel 34.4).

This is no comfortable message for pastors to hear: 'I am against the shepherds', says the Lord (Ezekiel 34.10). The official pastors are not exhorted, or admonished, or even threatened; they are actually sacked. God assumes sole personal charge of the flock, with a repeated and emphatic 'I'. 'I myself will search for my sheep, and will seek them out ... I will feed them with good pasture ... and I will make them lie down ... and I will bind up the injured, and I will strengthen the weak' (Ezekiel 34.11–16).

However, a few verses beyond the end of the passage we

heard tonight God extends this sole personal charge over the flock, with the promise of a human shepherd to come. 'I will set up over them one shepherd, my servant David, and he shall feed them: he shall feed them and be their shepherd' (Ezekiel 34.23). And so the good shepherd becomes a messianic prophecy.

Ezekiel's words recall the historical David, who was chosen as king against every expectation of the qualifications for kingship: he was the youngest son, and the one given the lowest job, that of keeping the sheep (1 Samuel 16.11). But beyond the first King David, the good shepherd becomes a messianic prophecy for another king from the line of David. When Jesus says in John 10, 'I am the good shepherd', he is saying, 'I am the one who speaks and acts in the name of God'.

So, as Ezekiel teaches us there is only one good shepherd – the Lord God – amid the unreliable pastors of the Old Testament, so too there is only one good shepherd – Jesus Christ, the son of David – amid the unreliable pastors of the Christian era. We are not the bishops' flock: we are God's flock, we are Christ's flock.

Others may help Christ in pastoral work, but we know our good shepherd from two things. First, we recognize the voice of the true shepherd: 'the sheep follow him because they know his voice' (John 10.4). Second, the true shepherd lays down his life for his sheep: 'the good shepherd lays down his life for the sheep . . . and I lay down my life for the sheep' (John 10.11, 15).

With these two criteria for true shepherding, those who I was describing as sheep who look down and are fed up, may feel a new freedom – a freedom that comes from knowing that they have only one shepherd, as they have only one father, as they have only one God. The sheep will recognize the voice of the one who feeds them. They will simply recognize the voice. And the sheep will trust the one who dies for them. You cannot fake the gift of a life. With this new liberation, this new confidence that they are looked after, the sheep will go in and out of the sheepfold freely, and find the pasture that they need (John 10.9).

How many bishops have given their lives for the flock, as our true shepherd Jesus gave his life for the flock? There are indeed some who have, and through the guidance of their example they have led the flock further along the paths of righteousness through their death than others have who are still alive.

One such was Archbishop Oscar Romero, shot dead for the style of his pastoring on 24 March 1980 (he was shot by a gunman on the orders of the founder of the Arena political party, which later came to power). Archbishop Oscar Romero is now hailed throughout El Salvador and far beyond as St Romero of the Americas. He has not been officially canonized, but the flock recognize his voice. Two weeks before his death Archbishop Romero said:

> I have often been threatened with death ... As pastor I am obliged, by divine command, to give my life for those I love, who are all Salvadoreans, even for those who are going to assassinate me ... You can say, if they come to kill me, that I forgive and bless those who do it. Hopefully they may realize that they will be wasting their time. A bishop will die, but the church of God, which is the people, will never perish.

There is one other shepherding passage that, given the season of the resurrection, we cannot forget today. In that beautiful resurrection story at the Sea of Galilee, John 21, Jesus sits on the beach in the early dawn next to Simon Peter and asks him three times, 'Do you love me?' (John 21.15, 16, 17). He replies, 'Yes, yes, yes, you know I love you.' And Jesus tells him, 'If you love me, feed my sheep.' In other words, if you love me, do something about it, care for those others who are dear to me.

In this Easter season of happiness, we may, perhaps, from time to time, feel drawn to tell Jesus that we love him. And then, whether we are bishop, or priest, or deacon, or chorister, or lay person, we may let ourselves hear his invitation, his challenge, in reply. 'If you love me, do something about it. If you love me, care for those others who are dear to me. If you love me, feed my sheep.'

CHAPTER TWENTY-FOUR

Elections and the Victory of God

Isaiah 57.14–21; Luke 18.9–14

When I was asked to preach on the parable of the Pharisee and the tax-collector, I had no idea I would be preaching three days after the general election. It is a parable with a profound teaching about the nature of true prayer, and I will turn to that shortly. But given the context of this dramatic moment in our nation's history, of shellshock or jubilation as the case may be, it is difficult to ignore the other allusions that leap out of the text and practically hit us over the head with their aptness. I hope I will not cause offence, for that is not my intent.

Rather, what has happened is a prime example of how our understanding of scripture is quite crucially influenced by the context of our lives. The text comes out of, and feeds into, our lives. Brazilian theologian Carlos Mesters says there is in scripture a text, a pre-text, and a con-text. It is not a matter of our lives distorting the text; it is more a matter of there being no such thing as the text and nothing but the text.

There is a theological point as well as a literary critical point. The Bible is the book of the salvation history of the people of God, and that salvation history is ongoing, just as the people of God are ongoing. It is our book, about the history of our family and with relevance to our present story.

Read the Bible in that way, and we have some hope of seeing something of what it is all about. At different moments of our people's history, different emphases will come to the fore, different insights emerge. But read it just as a book about another people at another time, and it remains distant and unchallenging. We will not then be pierced by the word of God which (in the words of the epistle to the Hebrews) 'is living and active, sharper than any two-edged sword, piercing until it divides soul from spirit, joints from marrow; it is able to judge the thoughts and intentions of the heart' (Hebrews 4.12).

So what happens when we read the parable of the Pharisee and the tax-collector in the context of having just had our general election? How does the sword pierce? Let us listen again.

The story is directed to

> some who trusted in themselves that they were righteous and regarded others with contempt. Two men went up to the temple to pray, one a Pharisee and the other a tax-collector. The Pharisee, standing by himself, was praying thus: 'God, I thank you that I am not like other people: thieves, rogues, adulterers . . .' (vv. 9–11)

How might we like to continue the list? Fiddlers? Lager louts? There has been plenty of abusive labelling in politics recently from both sides. Cowards? Incompetents? Promise-breakers? Barefaced liars? And Jesus' comment is: 'All who exalt themselves will be humbled, but all who humble themselves will be exalted' (Luke 18.14).

It is impossible not to remember the humbling of Thursday night. The multiple humbling, which in some cases seemed to hit hardest on those who were regarded as most self-exalting. And that cuts both ways, for after a number of years – perhaps five, perhaps ten, perhaps fifteen – the party that now is triumphant will have its turn of being humbled. The individual who achieves a personal triumph at one election lives on to endure a personal crushing at a later time.

Accepting such a defeat is not easy, because all power corrupts, and absolute power corrupts absolutely. We are built – we are all built – in such a way that giving up power is one of the hardest things in the world to do. Power is not something intrinsically bad: it is a force for good as well as a force for evil. And we tell ourselves that we want the power because of all the good we can do with it. That is rarely devoid of truth, but it is equally rarely the whole truth.

Knowing how far it is true and how far it is self-deception is the difficult bit. When am I a knight in a white suit, braving the fire of the sleaze-ridden snipers? And when am I an arrogant, interfering 'BBC journalist from Hampstead'? The first step to knowing which is which is wanting to know it, being open to the possibility, indeed the likelihood, of self-deception. And that is humility, which in the message of this parable, is the way to salvation. It is the way of the sinner who knew he was rubbish, and would not even look up to heaven.

Last Sunday in chapel I was struck by a similar message, from some very familiar words which can easily dull with repetition, but which cannot be heard in the context of an imminent general election without that quality of the sword slipping in between the ribs in a most uncomfortable manner. They are the words of the *Magnificat*:

> He has shown strength with his arm;
> he has scattered the proud in the thoughts of their hearts.
> He has brought down the powerful from their thrones,
> and lifted up the lowly;
> he has filled the hungry with good things,
> and sent the rich away empty. (Luke 1.51–3)

Hearing those words, which are such good news to the poor and marginalized, such bad news to the comfortable and established, I could not help but think: What is God's project for this country? Where would God's vote fall? There is not just one right answer. There are different views on how you achieve God's project. But the point is this: these are the right questions.

I promised to say something also about the parable's message on prayer. Again, this is intrinsically linked to the more topical thoughts that have grabbed the forefront of our attention, for it is all a matter of humility. The tax-collector in the parable has given us words which the Orthodox Church has taken for its famous Jesus prayer: 'God, be merciful to me, a sinner!' If we cannot say that, or if we think we have no need to say it, we are doomed. If we can say that, all the rest of salvation follows: 'this man went down to his home justified' (Luke 18.14).

Forgiveness follows, justification follows, reform follows, new life follows.

Humility is not a virtue of perfection, the icing on the cake for those who live decent, upright lives. It is both necessary, and sufficient, for salvation. And that is why the poor and despised, who are humble already, are at such an advantage when it comes to making their peace with God, and why the rich and powerful, whose lifestyle militates against humility, are at such a disadvantage. Not that being rich and powerful means you cannot be a good Christian, but it makes it much harder. It is harder to say, and mean it, 'God, be merciful to me, a sinner!'

When some Christians pray, they make speeches, explaining the wonderful plans for God they are carrying out, and asking that the right conditions be granted for their success. But God does not need to be informed of what we are doing for the gospel. God does not need to be persuaded to favour this or that enterprise. God's ways are not our ways, and it may be that God's will turns out to be the failure of a project undertaken for what we believed were the best of Christian motives. There is only one intention that we can be absolutely certain that God has for us, and that is that we should recognize that we are sinners and ask God's help for what we cannot overcome on our own.

'God, be merciful to me, a sinner.' It is the best of all prayers, the foundation for all prayers: the prayer that rids us of any need to speechify before God; the prayer that cleanses us and opens us up so that the grace of God can flood in; the prayer that prepares us, with the little bits of power and opportunity that we have, for the crushing moments of defeat that may in worldly terms be a humiliation but in God's terms are a gateway to a truer freedom.

'OK, we lost', said ousted Prime Minister John Major. But God did not lose. Never, since the first Easter Sunday when Christ rose from the dead; never, since the first Ascension day when he entered the fullness of his glory; never again need we fear that God will lose. And for our losses, our failures, our sins and our incompetences we need do nothing more than say 'God, be merciful to me, a sinner.' Then we can share in the victory of God.

When we meet to remember the mystery of Ascension, it is not our victory we will be celebrating. Even those who are enjoying a landslide victory today will be overthrown. It is God's victory, and that will never be overthrown.

CHAPTER TWENTY-FIVE

A Joyful Goodbye

Deuteronomy 34; John 16.12–24

The readings today speak of birth and death – the death of Moses and the saying of Jesus about the joy of childbirth. Why have these two readings been chosen for today, as we approach the end of the Easter season? I think it is because they look forward to Ascension Day. Both are readings about partings tinged with sadness.

The story of Moses' death is a poignant one. Here is one of the greatest leaders of all time, who has risked all for the sake of God's people, confronting the wrath of Pharaoh and leading the unruly and faithless mob for forty years through the desert, teaching them God's ways and listening to their endless moaning about how even their captivity in Egypt was better than the freedom he had won them. Now at last, after forty years, the people are on the brink of the promised land, they have just the Jordan to cross. And God tells Moses that he will never go in to claim this inheritance. He will die on the very brink.

This saintly figure is to pay the penalty for some small sin, some questionable failure to show God's holiness 'before the eyes of the Israelites' (Numbers 20.12). Moses begs God, 'Let me cross over to see the good land beyond the Jordan' (Deuteronomy 3.25). But God was angry and said 'Never speak to me of this matter again! Go up to the top of Pisgah, and look around you to the west, to the north, to the south, and to the east. Look well, for you shall not cross over this Jordan' (Deuteronomy 3.26–7). And later in the same book, God again tells Moses:

> Ascend this mountain of the Abarim, Mount Nebo ... and view the land of Canaan, which I am giving to the Israelites for a possession; you shall die there on the mountain that you ascend .... Although you may view the land from a distance, you shall not enter it. (Deuteronomy 32.49–50, 52)

And so Moses makes his own form of ascension. He dies with the sight of what he has always wanted and worked for, and will never now enjoy. He can only hand it on to others. Yet his final recorded words are not ones of sorrow and bitterness, but of gratitude and happiness.

> There is none like God, O Jeshurun,
> who rides through the heavens to your help,
> majestic through the skies ....
> Happy are you, O Israel! Who is like you,
> a people saved by the Lord .... (Deuteronomy 34.26, 29)

They are words that would make a fine text for the ascent of Christ through the skies as the Son of God.

Now we turn to the gospel reading, and hear Jesus saying: 'When a woman is in labour, she has pain, because her hour has come. But when her child is born, she no longer remembers the anguish because of the joy of having brought a human being into the world' (John 16.21).

Death and birth are, I believe, very close. They are both profoundly religious events when we touch the mystery of things and stand on the threshold of eternity. When a woman is in labour she feels great pain – probably worse pain than she has ever felt before, or perhaps will ever feel again, until her death. Many in our society choose an epidural injection in the spine that takes away all feeling, others take strong pain-killers like pethidine or breathe in a gas mixture, and others again are determined to let nothing come between them and the full thrust of this experience, so they practise natural methods of pain control through breathing and relaxation.

The sensations are what one woman described as becoming a burning bush. Yet just at the moment when they become quite unbearable the woman discovers that she is at the life-giving moment of pushing the baby out of her body. Women emerge from this experience of labour glowing with serenity and purpose.

And we know why. To be present as a new person comes into the world, to participate actively in the work of loving creation, to help in God's finest production of a human being, to see and touch, stroke and kiss and smell this new baby who is so fragile and warm and full of loveliness ... all this is to be overcome with a religious wonder and awe. Birth teaches us about God.

And that is the message of Jesus in today's gospel. Think of the powerful emotions that come with the birth of a child, he says. Well, it will be like that, and more so, when you see me as I really am.

For nearly forty days now we have lived the message of Easter, seeing him, little by little, more and more, as he really is. We have moved with the gospel characters from hesitant amazement and wonder to a deeper confidence that he is alive.

We have relived the trembling relief of Mary Magdalene, who wanted to take him in her arms and never let him go. We have relived the shamefaced happiness of the apostles, who had run away and thought they had lost him for ever, until he came back to them in the upper room without a word of reproach. We have relived the burning hearts of Cleopas and his partner, who broke bread with him one evening when they were tired and who were so refreshed by seeing him that they got up that hour and walked all the way back to Jerusalem. We have relived the awe-filled gratitude of those friends, on whom he breathed and said, 'As the Father has sent me, so I send you .... Receive the Holy Spirit' (John 20.21–2), and also the repentant faith of Thomas, whose words we wish to echo whenever we feel ourselves in the presence of Christ, 'My Lord and my God' (John 20.28). We have relived the excitement of Peter, who plunged into the sea to swim to Jesus so as to reach him just a minute or so before the others who were coming by boat. And finally, we have relived the quiet togetherness of those who breakfasted together and who did not even need to utter the question, 'Who are you?'

One more Easter appearance still awaits us: the Ascension. Christ will go ahead into his promised land and, unlike Moses, we have the confidence that one day we will follow him. We will see him again, as he promises us in John's gospel, or rather, we will see him for the first time. And on that day our joy in him, which may already be indescribable and glorious, will be forever complete.

CHAPTER TWENTY-SIX

Ascension Morning

Acts 1.1–11

Ascension Thursday is the moment in the church's year when we celebrate Christ taking on the heavenly glory that was his before the foundation of the world. At the moment when we would see him as he really is, he is snatched from our sight, for while we remain in this world, the glory is too much for us to bear. On this day the power and honour and victory of the resurrection reach their utmost peak.

Many people have a favourite time in the church's year. For me, that favourite time is today, the feast of the Ascension.

But the feast is often misunderstood. I once invited friends for a drink to celebrate the Ascension only to find that one of them, a good Christian, said he did not believe in it. What he meant, he explained, was that he did not believe Christ had ever left us. But that is to see the Ascension as a sad goodbye to the past, instead of a joyous greeting of the future, even if tinged with the depths and nostalgia that parting brings. It is the feast of the ascendancy of Christ, the day of his ultimate triumph.

If the feast is often misunderstood, it is even more often ignored. Exeter College, Oxford, is one of very few places where the Ascension is celebrated as a special, joyous occasion. There is a custom here of singing the praises of Christ at the top of the tower, early on the morning of Ascension Day. The worshippers assemble at the lodge shortly before 8.00 a.m. and climb up the staircase of the tower, till they reach a last section of ladder which brings them out on to the top, from where the dreamy, promised land of beautiful Oxford lies spread out below.

The fresh morning air lifts the eyes to the skies, as the

anthems focus the mind on the Ascension through the heavens. 'Today he ascends into heaven', the choir sings, *Coelos ascendit hodie*. It is as though the joy cannot be bounded by the walls and roof of the chapel but must break out into the open air. It is a moment of extraordinary freshness and beauty.

One reason why the Ascension is often misunderstood is because its artistic expressions are so inadequate. The traditional way of showing the Ascension in art is through two sweet little feet dangling down out of a cloud at the top of the picture. Rather than the two little feet, my preferred image of the Ascension is the way it was done in the Wintershall passion play (a sort of British Oberammegau event that takes place near Guildford). There, Jesus simply walked away around a huge lake, and our eyes followed him for a long time as he walked further into the distance. He was going to a place far from us, but we could feast our eyes on him all the way along the route.

Yet in art, the majesty of Christ, that theologically attaches to the Ascension, is more often painted in the context of the Last Judgement, as he returns in glory. It is another mystery shot through with the complexities of both triumph and pain. The Last Judgement and the Ascension should be seen as very close to each other, like two sides of one coin. As the angels say in the first chapter of Acts: 'This Jesus, who has been taken up from you into heaven, will come in the same way as you saw him go into heaven' (Acts 1.11).

According to Luke – Acts, there were forty days – mirroring the forty years of Moses in the wilderness – before the resurrection came to its full completion with the intimacy of Christ in the bosom of his Father in heaven. But it is hardly a time of sorrow – even as Jesus departs he promises the imminent gift of the Spirit that will come at Pentecost, or Whitsun. Even as he withdraws he leaves them with an image that will remain happily imprinted on their minds. 'He led them out as far as Bethany, and, lifting up his hands, he blessed them. While he was blessing them, he withdrew from them and was carried up into heaven' (Luke 24.50–1). That is not a sad farewell but a distancing, rich in blessings.

In John, by contrast, the Ascension appears much more tightly interwoven with the day of the resurrection. Jesus appears to Mary Magdalene on the very morning of his rising and tells her: 'Do not hold on to me, because I have not yet ascended to the Father. But go to my brothers and sisters and say to them, "I am ascending to my Father and your Father, to my God and your God"' (John 20.17).

To hold on to Jesus, to cling to him, to grieve at his parting would be as much a mistake as for parents to grieve at the wedding of their child. How can they be sad, even if their child is leaving their home to go and live elsewhere? They are happy because of the happiness of the child that they love. It is the same with the Ascension. Any sadness at Jesus' change of abode, from earth to heaven, is completely overshadowed by joy at his entry into his real, ultimate and eternal home, where he will be united with his Father and our Father, with his God and our God. His new family and new home is pledged to us for the future as our family and home.

Earlier in the Easter season I spoke about the words of Jesus to Peter, the shepherd and pastor, at the end of John's gospel, words that are addressed also to us: 'Do you love me?' It may seem odd to others if we say we love a character from history whom we have never seen, and yet it is our experience. As the first epistle of Peter puts it so well and so simply: 'Although you have not seen him, you love him; and even though you do not see him now, you believe in him and rejoice with an indescribable and glorious joy' (1 Peter 1.8).

We are embarrassed to speak of that love of Jesus too openly, and yet it nestles discreetly in our hearts. That love of Jesus is the reason for our happiness at his happiness in his Ascension. He rises over all things; he goes up in triumph; he enters into the fullness of God's glory. And because we love him, nothing could make us happier than that.

PENTECOST AND BEYOND

CHAPTER TWENTY-SEVEN

Pentecost Thoughts

John 14.8–17, 25–7; Acts 2.1–21

Ten days ago we celebrated a glorious Ascension day, in the fresh early morning sun. Tonight, on a peaceful summer evening, we remember the feast of Pentecost. Glory and peace, the themes of this season.

Glory. Jesus says in today's gospel reading that the Father is '*glorified* in the Son' (John 14.13, emphasis added) – a wonderful gesture towards the triumph of Jesus' ascendancy. There are portents in the heavens, says Joel in the passage quoted in Acts, 'before the coming of the Lord's great and *glorious* day' (Acts 2.20, emphasis added; cf. Joel 2.31). This is a prophecy of the day of Pentecost. It is always easier to feel glorious when the weather is good, and we have been blessed this year with great weather for both the Ascension and Pentecost.

Peace. Jesus promises peace as his parting gift. In today's gospel reading, he says 'Peace I leave with you; my peace I give to you' (John 14.27). And in John's account of the giving of the Spirit, which happens not on the feast of Pentecost after the Ascension but on Easter Sunday evening when Jesus comes to his disciples in the upper room, again 'peace' is his message. 'Peace be with you', he says twice, and he breaths on them the gift of the Spirit (John 20.21–2). 'Breath' and 'Spirit' and 'wind' are all the same word in Hebrew and in Greek.

Glory and peace. Glory – the heights of drama, the violent sound of wind, the flash of fire, the moon turning to blood, the explosion of language, thoughts and experiences so powerful that they force their way out into language after language, as though one tongue alone is inadequate to express the excitement of the message of Jesus.

And peace – the end of fear, misunderstanding, inner turmoil and anxiety; the quiet of conscience for those who have fled from or denied their Lord, or refused to believe in him. Doubting Thomas refused to believe, but he too is given the same greeting, 'Peace be with you' (John 20.26). The quiet of conscience is a gift to spread to others, for the gift of the Spirit is the power given to the church to forgive the sins of others: 'If you forgive the sins of any, they are forgiven them' (John 20.23). There is no peace like the peace of conscience.

How much our generation needs these gifts of the Spirit, glory and peace, in contrast to the twin ills of dullness and anxiety.

Dullness. How desperately people look for thrills and excitement – drugs, sex, rave, speed – because they are bored and want to break through the dullness and flatness of their lives. And they *should* want to break through the dullness and flatness of their lives. Our faith is an exciting faith. God preserve us from drab religion.

Anxiety. How frequently people are broken down by worries, drilled through with depression, tormented by jealousies or fears. We *should* seek a consolation from those things that trouble us. Our faith is a consoling faith. There are many ways of translating the Greek word 'paraclete' from John 14.26, which literally means someone you call to your side, but among the translations used are 'consoler', 'comforter', 'helper', 'intercessor', 'advocate'. God preserve us from a miserable religion of niggles and scruples and guilt.

With those two gifts of glory and peace, the one stressing the joyful climaxes, the other the underlying calm, Pentecost is the day of all days when it is appropriate to say, 'I am so happy.' We don't often hear those words said, but whenever we do we sense a touch of the Holy Spirit. People say it, perhaps, when they get the university place they want, or a job they long for, or become engaged to the person they love. When Louise Woodward, the English au pair girl in the USA, was cleared of murdering the baby boy in her charge, her sister said again and again to the television cameras, 'I am so happy.'

Pentecost is the feast when the objective victory of the resurrection, and the triumph of the Ascension, takes such deep root in our hearts that the glory and peace is no longer something that we see and hear without and try to take within, but rather something that has become so strong within us that it pours out of us again – unlimited, unqualified, unstoppable, bursting all the communications barriers.

I end with some words from Teilhard de Chardin's 'Mass on the World', which beautifully draws together the fire of Pentecost with the eucharist, in an evocation of the glory of creation and the peace of redemption.

> Blazing Spirit, Fire . . . Radiant Word . . . pronounce over this earthly travail your twofold efficacious word . . . Over every living thing which is to spring up, to grow, to flower, to ripen . . . say again the words: This is my Body. And over every death-force which waits in readiness to corrode, to wither, to cut down, speak again your commanding words which express the supreme mystery of faith: This is my Blood. It is done. Once again, the Fire has penetrated the earth.

CHAPTER TWENTY-EIGHT

More Pentecost Thoughts

Acts 2

It is easy to feel a certain sense of let-down about Pentecost, otherwise known as Whitsun. Here is one of the greatest feasts of the Christian year, some say the third greatest after Easter and Christmas, a time of fire and wind and enthusiasm. We can feel a bit of a failure if we don't feel, on this day each year, a new burst of the Holy Spirit pulsing through us. We can feel we have missed out if we do not share the sense evoked by Janet Morley in her Pentecost prayer:

> Flame dancing Spirit, come,
> Sweep us off our feet and
> Dance us through our days.
> Surprise us with your rhythms;
> Dare us to try new steps, explore
> New patterns and new partnerships;
> Release us from old routines
> To swing in abandoned joy and
> Fearful adventure. And
> In the intervals,
> Rest us
> In your still centre. Amen.
> (*The New Women Included*, The St Hilda Community,
>   SPCK, 1996)

That is a marvellous prayer. Are we feeling that sense of the Spirit racing through our souls? I hope we are a bit. But I want to say that it does not matter if we are not. Rather than feeling a

new wind of the Spirit, it can be more important to recall an old
one.

There have been times in our life, no doubt, when we have
felt something of that racing excitement, that energy that made
us capable of deeds we could not do before. We all have had
such moments, and some of us have particularly had such
moments in our Christian faith – a day when the Spirit filled us,
a moment when God touched us with an inexplicable grace, a
time when we took Christ into our hearts, a turning point of our
faith commitment.

But for other Christians there has been no identifiable
moment when they received the Spirit. For them it has been a
gradual growth, a steady consolidation. Many people who find
the practice of charismatic prayer offputting rather than
liberating can feel particularly flat at Pentecost.

What I want to do today is to show how the story from
Acts is not just about feeling fantastic, but about something
more important. I want to show that there is a better test of
whether we have really received the Spirit than that of
emotion.

The Holy Spirit that is given today is one which breaks
through the accustomed barriers of marginalization and discrimination in three identifiable ways. The Spirit breaks across
barriers of language; the Spirit breaks across barriers of sex; and
the Spirit breaks across barriers of race. If our lives are devoted
to breaking across those barriers, then we too may be said to
have received the Spirit.

The Spirit breaks down the barriers of language. The gift of
tongues, in this account from Acts, is not just the uninhibited
babble of joy in the Lord that is often called the gift of tongues.
It is a gift for communication between people of different
languages. The followers of Jesus are able to speak to those of
other languages and to be understood. They are not understood
in the way a foreigner understands us if we speak to them slowly
with articulation, but they are understood in the way a
foreigner understands us if we speak to them in their language,
not in ours.

We share in this tradition of Pentecost when we learn the
languages of others, when we make the step towards them,

placing ourselves at the disadvantage of trying to communicate in a tongue which is not our mother tongue, instead of placing them at that disadvantage. Learning the language of another is for most of us a costly and lengthy process.

This is a lesson which we English-speakers particularly need to learn. We are so used to others taking that step towards us, freeing us of the need to take that step towards them. All nations with imperialist histories have this advantage which lasts for generation after generation – the Romans, the British, the Spanish, the Portuguese, the French, the Germans, the Russians .... No one likes to speak the language of the oppressor, but in the end they have to. Pentecost reminds us to stop expecting others to speak our language because we used to have an empire. Instead let us learn theirs.

A missionary priest once said to me that when you learn a language you go through the process of childhood again; you become a little child, struggling to say simple things clumsily, excluded from the conversations of others, unable either to speak or to understand. Only gradually, over years, do you grow up, and become someone who is taken seriously, able to participate. When you are not speaking your mother tongue you are always at a disadvantage, but at a disadvantage that slowly narrows as you continue committing yourself to that step towards others.

The sudden gift of tongues at Pentecost is there to encourage us of the worth of the enterprise, not to discourage us because we cannot do it instantly as they did. Just as the nurse and the doctor and the therapist share in the healing ministry of Jesus, even though their healing may be slow and partial rather than a sudden miracle, so too the student of languages shares in the gift and work of the Holy Spirit. For the Spirit breaks down the barriers of language.

The Spirit breaks down the barriers of sex. In Acts 1 we are told who spent those days after the Ascension in the upper room, praying and waiting for the baptism of the Spirit that Jesus had promised them before he ascended. Those in the upper room included the twelve – Peter, John, James and Andrew, Philip and Thomas, Bartholomew and Matthew, James son of Alphaeus and Simon the Zealot, and Judas son of

James – 'together with certain women, including Mary the mother of Jesus, as well as his brothers' (Acts 1.14).

So often the Bible forgets to mention the presence of women, so that people sometimes think that if women are not mentioned they are not there – a false conclusion, if we remember that embarrassing giveaway line from the miracle of the loaves: 'there were five thousand, not including the women and the children' (Matthew 14.21).

Now at Pentecost it is as though the Good News of human equality has finally broken through to make up for the omissions of the past, for women are mentioned explicitly. Not only does the writer of Acts remember the women, but so does the prophet Joel, who is quoted. Joel goes out of his way to say that women are prophets: 'I will pour out my Spirit upon all flesh, and your sons *and your daughters* shall prophesy .... Even upon my slaves, both men *and women*, in those days I will pour out my Spirit, and they shall prophesy' (Acts 2.17–18 emphasis added, cf. Joel 2.28–9).

The iconographical tradition of the church also remembers women at Pentecost, or at least Mary, the mother of Jesus, who in painting after painting is placed in the dominant position at the centre of the Twelve as the tongues of fire pour down from heaven. It is so, to take two out of many examples, in the famous Maestà cycle of Duccio in Siena, and in the Pentecost painted by El Greco that hangs in the Prado in Madrid.

But Acts 1.14 tells us Mary was only one of the women in that group, so when art shows her as the only woman we must take her as a symbol for the presence of the other women. She stands both for those who were historically there in the upper room, and for those who through the centuries and in our own day are called by God to play an equal role as recipients of the Spirit, as prophets, as speakers, as communicators of the gospel.

Women at Pentecost are no longer the silent, invisible, unmentioned supporters of the men. They receive the Spirit not in order to feel equal but different and sit modestly in a corner but, according to Joel, in order to prophesy. They receive the gift of the Spirit not in order to go home and do the cooking and look after the children but, according to Jesus, in order to 'be my witnesses in Jerusalem, in all Judea and

Samaria, and to the ends of the earth' (Acts 1.8). That is the mission to which women, and men, are called on this day of Pentecost, when the Spirit breaks down the barriers of sex.

The Spirit breaks down the barriers of race. Recently I was in Rome for the conclusion of the African Synod, and I was aware, once again, of the pride African Christians take in their ancestry. We tend to think and speak of the churches of Africa as new churches, and to treat them somewhat as novices, even as naive. But Africans are keen to notice and to point out their ancient Christian roots. The Ethiopian eunuch, baptized by Philip in Acts 8 (v. 38), was an African. Simon of Cyrene, who had the privilege of helping bear the cross of Jesus, was an African: he gives his name to the Simon of Cyrene Institute for black theology in London. And here in Acts 2 we read that the original crowd of Pentecost converts included Africans: those who heard the disciples preaching to them in their own languages, included people from 'Egypt and the parts of Libya belonging to Cyrene' (Acts 2.10).

It is so easy to overlook points of detail like this, hidden in seemingly boring lists, but if you are an African you notice. If you are an African, no matter which corner of Africa you come from, you are likely to trace the roots of civilization back, not to ancient Greece and Rome, but to ancient Egypt. Here at Pentecost we see that Africans were in on the very foundation of Christianity, part of that day that is called the birthday of the church, and that is very much more than anything the British can claim as their ancient Christian roots. The Spirit breaks down the barriers of race, and dispels the myth that the faith has to come through Europe before it reaches the other continents of the world.

So at Pentecost we take to ourselves the gift of the Spirit, not only by leaping for joy and breaking forth into praise but, far more deeply and profoundly, by living lives that break down the barriers of language, of sex and of race.

I want to end with the image of the tongue of flame on the head, which is the image of a Christian as a lighted candle. One such lighted candle in our generation was a Spanish Jesuit poet called Luis Espinal, who was tortured and murdered in Bolivia on 21 March 1980 for his work in the media on behalf of the marginalized. His work was on behalf of those, we could say, who stood on the wrong side of the barriers of language and of sex and of race. Before he knew that he would be killed for his Christian commitment, he wrote this passage, which can stand as a fitting comment on the quiet but authentic meaning of Pentecost:

> We are candles that only have meaning if we are burning, for only then do we serve our purpose of being light ... Losing one's life should not be accompanied by pompous or dramatic gestures. Life is to be given simply, without fanfare, like a waterfall, like a mother nursing her child, like the humble sweat of the sower of seed.
>
> Train us, Lord, and send us out to do the impossible, because behind the impossible is your grace and your presence; we cannot fall into the abyss. The future is an enigma; our journey leads us through the fog; but we want to go on giving ourselves because you are waiting there in the night, in a thousand human eyes brimming over with tears. (*A New Way of Being Church: Interviews and Testimonies from Latin America Press*, Lima, 1984, p. 36)

On this day of Pentecost, may God send us out, into this night, and into the fog of the future, to seek out those who suffer discrimination; and by the power of the Spirit may their eyes come to brim over not with tears of sorrow but with tears of joy.

CHAPTER TWENTY-NINE

Understanding the Trinity

Isaiah 6.1–8; Psalm 29; Revelation 4

Today, the first Sunday after Pentecost, is Trinity Sunday. The Trinity is a precious doctrine for Christians and, indeed, is often taken as the benchmark of Christian orthodoxy. That may be puzzling for several reasons.

One is that it is a hard doctrine to understand or even to see the point of, especially in a religion that places such stress on there being only one God.

It could also be argued that of all the Christian doctrines, this is the one that sounds most patriarchal, because Father and Son are both masculine analogies, even though (as Jerome pointed out) the word for Spirit is 'feminine in Hebrew, masculine in Latin and neuter in Greek, for there is no sex in the divinity' (*In Esaiam*, 4, 40, 9–11).

Another reason why we might be puzzled at the importance given to the doctrine of the Trinity is that the term never occurs once in scripture. The nearest we come to it is in the mission charge at the end of Matthew, when the disciples are sent out to baptize 'in the name of the Father and of the Son and of the Holy Spirit' (Matthew 28.19). But that threefold formula, as such, occurs nowhere else in the Bible.

Why, then, does the doctrine of the Trinity matter so much to Christians? I will share with you some suggestions.

I suggest that the Trinity, the idea of Father, Son and Spirit, is almost the name of our God: it is the term by which we can recognize the Christian God. Now of course there is only one God (even if in three persons), so everyone who believes in God, by whatever name, believes in the same God, because there is none other. Yet in each religion this one God has a slightly different character, as we reach towards an understanding of the supreme being. People feel possessive about God's names – Yahweh, or Abba, or Allah – just as people feel possessive and respectful about the names of anyone they know and love. 'Father, Son and Spirit': we know that God, we trust that God. This is the God of Jesus, the God of the early church.

Conversely, people take offence when the names of their friends or family are mis-spelt or garbled, and Christians often feel defensive when the God they know is referred to in an unfamiliar way. One example: the Orthodox still, to this day, feel deeply offended by the way the western church inserted into the Creed, without consulting the universal church, the word *Filioque*, meaning 'and from the Son'. The full phrase now is, 'I believe in the Holy Spirit who proceeds from the Father and the Son'. The Orthodox feel this is not the God they know.

And they maintain – quite possibly rightly, for the Orthodox have a richer devotion to the Spirit than we do – that the insertion of the word *Filioque* has led to an undermining of a balanced Trinitarian faith. Western Christians paint the Trinity as an old man, a young man and a bird flying out somewhere from the middle of them – leading to the ironic taunt 'Hunt the pigeon' for this tradition of Trinitarian iconography. The Orthodox prefer to base their icon of the Trinity on the equal, triangular relationship of the three divine visitors who came to Abraham and Sarah by the oaks of Mamre in Genesis 18.

Another reason for the importance of the Trinity is that although Unitarianism (the claim that there are not three persons in the godhead but only one) sounds very attractive at first, because it stresses that there is only one God, it is hard to reconcile with faith in Jesus. If the Son, the second person of the Trinity, is not God, then why do we worship him? There is a world of difference between admiring Jesus, and saying to Jesus, as Thomas did, 'My Lord and my God' (John 20.28).

Why, then, not stick with two persons, Father and Son, remembering that the Spirit is in any case referred to frequently in the New Testament as the Spirit of Jesus? Perhaps because there is something flat about it, something two-dimensional.

Living as we do in the world of matter, of three dimensions, we can see that a threefold God is more able to fill the universe.

Moreover, living as we do in the world of human relationships, we can see that a threefold God is a community – not just a couple who gaze into each other's eyes in mutual self-absorption, but a relationship of love that is fruitful and goes beyond itself. Again I am reminded of the Orthodox icon of three figures sitting around a table to eat, where there is a holiness about the space between them.

What, then, can we say about the weak witness of scripture to Trinitarian doctrine? We can say that the Trinity is a truth about God that emerged slowly, a doctrine that was just beginning to form as the New Testament was written. But it is implicit in the Johannine discourses about 'the Father and I are one' (such as John 10.30), and in the promise to send the Paraclete or Advocate (John 15.26) – passages that are associated with the feast of Pentecost. Pentecost leads on to Trinity Sunday in a natural progression.

That progression out of Pentecost, which progresses out of the Ascension, which progresses out of the Resurrection, puts Trinitarian belief full-square in the context of glory – a theme on which I preached at Pentecost. Tonight's two readings give great prominence to the theme of glory in the way they present God. 'The whole earth is full of his glory' cry the seraphim to Isaiah (Isaiah 6.3). The twenty-four elders of Revelation 4 declare 'You are worthy, our Lord and God, to receive glory' (Revelation 4.11).

This is far from the only point in common between the Old and New Testament readings tonight. The two readings are quite astonishingly similar.

In both we have a vision of God sitting on a throne, very glorious to see. In Isaiah the hem of God's robe fills the temple and the house is filled with smoke. In Revelation God looks like jasper and carnelian and around the throne is a rainbow that looks like an emerald. Meanwhile there come from the throne flashes of lightning and rumblings of thunder, just as in Psalm 29 'the God of glory thunders' and 'the voice of the Lord flashes forth flames of fire' (Psalm 29.3, 7).

Another similarity is that both Isaiah and Revelation include the threefold, Trinitarian cry 'Holy, holy, holy', which becomes the basis for the Sanctus that is sung in the Mass.

The passage from Isaiah has always been a particular favourite of mine. I love the rhythm of the verses and the breathtakingly majestic atmosphere, with its evocation of incense, and its cathartic purging of sin with a burning coal. Seeing the glory of God leads us to feel our own littleness, deeply aware of the gulf between God's great goodness and our petty, selfish sinfulness.

The purging of our guilt by God's power, as by a burning coal, propels us into mission. 'Whom shall I send?' says God, and Isaiah cries with joy, 'Here I am, send me!' It is all reminiscent of the mission charge at the end of Matthew – the 'Father, Son and Holy Spirit' text – where the sight of the glorious Christ on a mountain in Galilee drives the disciples to worship and leads to them being sent out in mission to all nations.

A vision of glory, a mission to the world. Such was also the experience of Ignatius of Loyola, founder of the Jesuits, when he had his revelation of the Trinity. He tells it in his own words, referring to himself in the third person:

> One day, while praying the office of Our Lady on the steps of the above-mentioned monastery, his understanding began to be raised up, in that he was seeing the Most Holy Trinity in the form of three keys on a keyboard, and this with so many tears and so many sobs that he could not control himself. And on walking that morning in a procession which was leaving from there, at no point could he restrain his tears until the mealtime, nor after the meal could he stop talking, only about the Most Holy Trinity, and this with many comparisons, a great variety of them, as well as much relish and consolation, in such a way that the impression has remained with him for the whole of his life, and he feels great devotion when praying to the Most Holy Trinity. (*Autobiography*, 28, in *Saint Ignatius of Loyola: Personal Writings*, trans. Joseph A. Munitiz and Philip Endean, Penguin Classics, 1996)

Whenever I feel I cannot see the point of the Trinity, I

remember that account by Ignatius, where his vision of the Trinity as a chord of music is so strong that he cannot doubt it.

A similarly powerful vision was had by the woman who founded the women's equivalent of the Jesuits, Mary Ward. Here is Mary Ward's account of her revelation. It has a Trinitarian quality in the threefold 'glory, glory, glory' (like 'holy, holy, holy'), and again, it is intrinsically linked to a vision of the mission she must take up:

> While dressing ... I was brushing my hair at the mirror, [when] something very supernatural befell me ... I was abstracted out of my whole being, it was shown to me with clarity and certainty that I was not to be of the order of St Teresa but some other thing was determined for me, without all comparison more to the glory of God than my entrance into that holy religious order. I did not see what the assured good thing would be but the glory of God which was to come through it showed itself inexplicably and so abundantly as to fill my soul in such a way that I remained for a good space without feeling or hearing anything but the sound: GLORY, GLORY, GLORY. All appeared to last but a moment: afterwards I realised it must have been two hours.
> (*A World to Tell, a Life to Live: Mary Ward, Her Own Story*, William Hewett, 1985)

Inspired by all those Trinitarian visions – Isaiah's and the book of Revelation's, Ignatius's and Mary Ward's – let our prayer be that our eyes be open to God's glory, that our unworthiness be cleansed by God's mercy, and that our lives be turned to God's service. 'Here I am, send me!'

We make this prayer in the name of the Trinity, however we best may understand or articulate the mystery. In the name of God: Life-giver, Pain-bearer, Love-maker. In the name of God: Shelter, Shepherd, Sustainer. In the name of God: Father, Son and Holy Spirit. Amen.

CHAPTER THIRTY

The Glory of God

Exodus 33.7–23; John 2.1–11

> He revealed his glory, and his disciples believed in him.
> (John 2.11)

The marriage of Cana is about far more than the point typically made at weddings, that Jesus blessed marriage by his presence. For John, the only evangelist to include this miracle, the miracle at Cana is a mysterious pointer to the eucharist.

I say mysterious, because John's gospel is the only one not to include the institution of the eucharist at the Last Supper. Over that moment he draws a veil, as something too holy to be exposed to public gaze. But he shows his eucharistic faith in other significant clues that would be picked up by the early Christians, initiated into the sacred mysteries: by the sign of water and blood from the side of Christ on the cross (baptism and the eucharist); by the eucharistic discourse after the feeding of the five thousand ('my flesh is true food and my blood is true drink' John 6.55); and by the miracle at Cana when he turned water into wine – just as later he would turn wine into blood – in 'the first of his signs', which 'revealed his glory' (John 2.11). Glory is a sign of divinity. As John says in his prologue: 'We have seen his glory, the glory as of a father's only son, full of grace and truth' (John 1.14).

The Old Testament reading speaks of that glory of the divinity in dramatically powerful terms. At the very end of the Pentateuch (the first five books of the Bible, which form a single section leading up to the crossing into the promised land) we are told how special Moses was – not just a very great mystic but a uniquely great one in Israel's history. 'Never since has there arisen a prophet in Israel like Moses, whom the Lord knew face to face' (Deuteronomy 34.10).

This picks up the phrase from today's reading, 'The Lord used to speak to Moses face to face, as one speaks to a friend' (Exodus 33.11). The chapter tells how Moses used to go to pray in the tent of meeting, where a pillar of cloud would stand guard at the entrance, and how Moses begged God, 'Show me your glory' (Exodus 33.18). As the story progresses we hear of a mystical experience so powerful that when, one chapter further on, Moses has finished communing with God, 'the skin of his face shone because he had been talking with God' (Exodus 34.29). So striking was this that Aaron and the other Israelites were afraid to come near him, and Moses had to hide the shining of his face with a veil.

What is this mystical experience that Moses had? Who is this God whom Moses came to know? It is often said by theologians that God has two opposing qualities held in balance – transcendence and immanence. Transcendence refers to the greatness of God, the glory of God that is unspeakable, beyond any human comprehension. Immanence refers, on the contrary, to the closeness of God, the intimacy of divine life that is within all things. God is far and near; mind-blowing in his greatness, inescapable in his closeness. That is why this passage from Exodus 33 is such a tremendous one, because it captures both aspects of God.

God, in his immanence, speaks to Moses as one speaks to a friend, with intimacy, in a whisper. Many of the recorded prayer experiences of Moses have that quality of centring again and again, in a rather inconsequential mystical rambling, around an inexpressible experience of God's presence, as Moses meditates around the themes of 'I know and love you, let me know and love you; you know and love me, let me be known and loved by you.' Roughly, the prayer dialogue of Exodus 33 goes like this:

God says, 'I know you by name. You have found favour in my sight.'

Moses says, 'If I have found favour in your sight, show me your ways. Then I may know you and find favour in your sight.'

God says, 'My presence will go with you, and I will give you rest.'

Moses says, 'How shall it be known that I have found favour in your sight, unless you go with us?'

God says, 'You have found favour in my sight. I know you by name.'

Moses says, 'Show me your glory I pray.'

God says, 'I will make all my goodness pass before you. I will proclaim my name before you. But you cannot see my face. No one shall see me and live.'

And then in an exquisitely anthropomorphic metaphor – that is a metaphor that speaks of God as though in human shape – God places his hand over Moses' eyes until he has passed, so that Moses sees God's back but not his face. In other words, the immanence of God's protective care keeps Moses safe while the transcendent power of God passes by, so tremendous that no one can see it and live.

In this life-consuming power of God we have an echo of a phrase used a few chapters earlier, when 'the appearance of the glory of God was like a devouring fire on the top of the mountain' (Exodus 24.17).

The nearest we can come to expressing the contemplative enjoyment between God and Moses is to say it is the conversation of lovers. When you are in love with someone you just like to gaze on them: the very sight of the beloved fills you with delight. When someone is in love with you, you feel enormously graced that you have found favour in their sight, and that you give them pleasure simply by being there to gaze upon. And so it is with Moses and God. 'You have found favour in my sight.' They speak face to face, and God shows himself to Moses. This is contemplation, and it is sometimes called the prayer of simple regard, which means the prayer of just looking.

When you are in love, the name of your lover is something you dwell on. You doodle it on your notepad in idle moments. If you are one of Shakespeare's lovers, you may have the vandalizing habit of carving the beloved name on trees. You murmur it to yourself when you think no one is listening. You mutter it in your sleep. And so it is with Moses and God: 'I know you by name . . . I will proclaim before you my name.'

The revelation that Moses receives is of pure goodness: 'I will make all my goodness pass before you' says God. It is a revelation of mercy, allied with complete freedom: 'I will be gracious to whom I will be gracious, and will show mercy on whom I will show mercy' (Exodus 33.19). If mercy and goodness belong more to immanence and intimacy, there can be little comfort in that without the transcendent power as well. God's sheer goodness would be useless if it were not an all-powerful goodness. The question is, what is the most powerful force in the world? And the answer is, goodness is.

That is the sheer joy of the Judeo-Christian belief in God: that goodness is all-powerful. The greatest power in the universe is that of loving goodness. Goodness wins. Wins over all else. That terrifying and wondrous moment of Moses in the cleft of the rock, shielded by God's hand, is an affirmation that God is both good and great, both great and good.

The supremacy of good breaks through once again, definitively, in the resurrection of Jesus over all the worst that sin and death can do. Love is stronger than death. God is stronger than all the powers of destruction.

'I believe in God', we say in the Creed. God reveals his glory, and the disciples believe. To believe in God is to believe that the greatest power in the universe is good. To see God is to see that goodness shining forth so radiantly that you are consumed by it. To love God and be loved by God is to be held in the sheer delight of just looking at God, even at God's 'back', and to be overwhelmed by gratitude that you too find 'favour in God's sight', so that God delights in looking at you.

To say 'I believe in God' is to be marked by the memory of Moses sheltering in the cleft of the rock, seeing the ultimate reality of the universe, and radiating for ever afterwards the glory of the vision.

Index of Biblical Texts